THIRTY
of
FORTY
in the
49TH

**Memories of a
Wildlife Biologist in Alaska**

Robin L. West

Thirty of Forty in the 49th
Memories of a Wildlife Biologist in Alaska

©2020 Robin West

print ISBN: 978-1-09834-808-3
ebook ISBN: 978-1-09834-809-0

CONTENTS

FOREWORD

This book is a compilation of stories of life, work, and play in the Last Frontier: Alaska. It includes accounts of my career with the U.S. Fish and Wildlife Service from 1978 to 2009 (30 of the 35 years that I worked for the federal government), and a later, specific trip on the Upper Yukon River, several years after retirement in 2019—40 years from when I had first visited the area.

Alaska was not a place I ever imagined I would visit, let alone work for the bulk of my career. Growing up in Grants Pass, Oregon, in the 1960s, I had never flown on a jet, the internet was yet to be invented, and neither video streaming nor cable television was available in our daily lives to help educate and motivate us—good, bad, or indifferent. My knowledge of the 49th state was what little came from reading the encyclopedia set that held a cherished place on our bookshelf and from what I had seen in a movie that was shown (for a fee) at our local fairgrounds. I was intrigued, however, with science and wild animals, and I loved hunting, fishing, and visiting wild places—the wilder the better. My goal in going to college to become a wildlife biologist was only to work somewhere with critters. While Alaska was not on my radar, when the opportunity came to go north to work after receiving my degree in Wildlife Science, I jumped at the chance. I bought a one-way ticket on Western Airlines to Anchorage and packed the bulk of my belongings into 2 suitcases, 2 cardboard apple boxes, a backpack, and a rifle case. I never regretted it.

ACKNOWLEDGMENTS
AND DISCLAIMER

My work accomplishments, career opportunities, and my very safety and survival, when frequently working in remote locations, all depended on others, too many to list, but I do want to mention a few: Gary Hickman, who hired me for my first job in Alaska, sight unseen, after I graduated from Oregon State University in 1978, and who worked to get me a permanent position with the U.S. Fish and Wildlife Service in 1980; Howard Metsker, one of my first supervisors and who introduced me to the Upper Yukon River and taught me much about living and working in the Bush Alaska; Jerry Stroebele, another supervisor during my early working days, a Vietnam combat veteran, and one of the kindest human beings I have ever known; Mike Smith, another supervisor, pilot, and friend; Glenn Elison, fellow manager, supervisor, and sharer of many adventures; deputy refuge managers, Mark Chase, Jim Hall, and Doug Staller, who faithfully gave me wonderful support when I was the manager of Kenai National Wildlife Refuge for 14 years; and Robyn Thorson, sharer of Alaska adventures during her own two tours there, mentor as Regional Director in Portland at the time of my retirement, and supplier of the desk from which I am recording these memories (as well as many other thoughtful gifts—especially chocolates from her talented sister)! Finally, I want to thank my beautiful wife, Shannon. This book is dedicated to her—no one could have supported my work and personal pursuits in Alaska more than her, and she did so whether it was going back to school, holding down a job, packing up and moving to a new remote location, or raising three children—more often than not with me somewhere other than at home.

The book is non-fiction; it is a compilation of my memories. While many of the events and recollections have components that are legal, political, or historic in nature (and all of the people and places are real), some folks may remember things differently. That is fine—they can write their own book.

There's a land where the mountains are nameless,

And the rivers all run God knows where;

There are lives that are erring and aimless,

And deaths that just hang by hair;

There are hardships than nobody reckons;

There are valleys unpeopled and still;

There's a land—oh, it beckons and beckons,

And I want to go back—and I will.

. . . .

From, *The Spell of the Yukon*—Robert W. Service

All Photographs are by the author or courtesy U.S. Fish and Wildlife Service archives

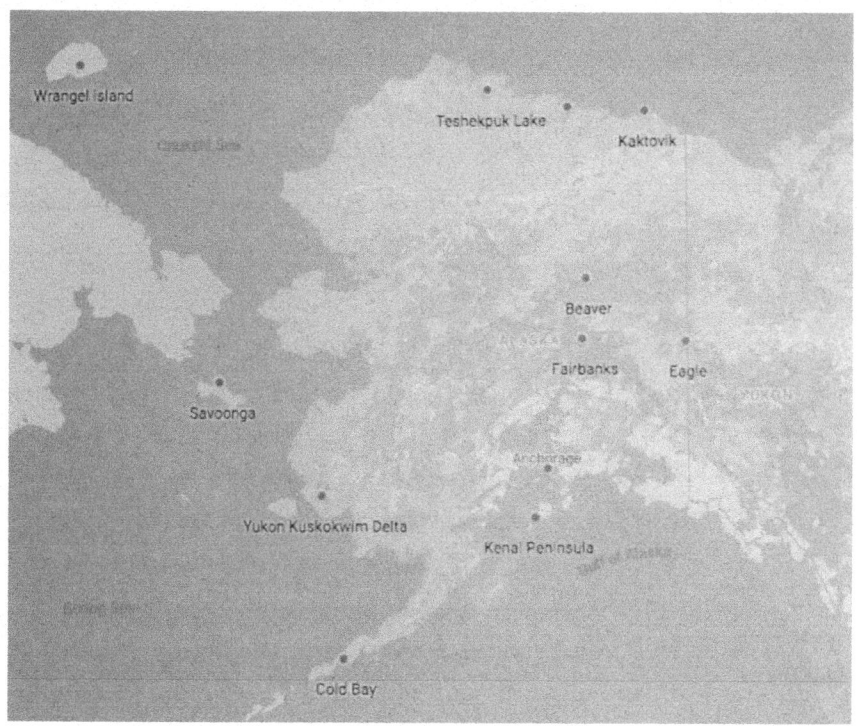

The author at Eagle, Alaska, 40 years after his first visit there.

Chapter One:

BACK ON THE RIVER AGAIN

July 13, 2019 – Canoe loaded, I waved a farewell of thanks to "my ride" (my oldest daughter Alex and her husband Jay) as I pushed off the beach at the boat landing above Eagle, Alaska. I dipped the paddle and pulled a J-stroke to propel me downstream in a straight line toward the looming bluff that rose above the Yukon River below the small town. I was struck by the similarities of a similar embarkation 40 years ago, July 1979: the sweeping expanse of brown water ahead, the intense sunshine of the mid-day in the broad river valley, and the striking bluffs on the horizon. Something was different though too—I did not hear the swirling of silt pushing against the vessel's hull. Perhaps the difference was attributable to the boat material— previously aluminum and now a composite plastic? Or, perhaps my hearing had faded enough that such subtle sounds were now lost to me. This thought made me aware of other differences. Previously I was in my early twenties and the trip was the first of what would lead to thousands of miles traveled by raft and canoe, and many hundreds of nights spent in a tent in the far north. I was enthusiastic then for sure, but green (I would have been rightly labelled a "cheechako"). Now, needing reading glasses to see a map and with flexibility reduced to where getting over the aches from a day's paddling was taking noticeably longer to fade, I was feeling my age. A good start to a day now, I mused, is one in which I didn't need to sit down in order to put on my socks. I thought too though, along with the less desirable changes that came with aging, the passing years also offered the benefit of experience.

Experience brings confidence, confidence provides a relaxed attitude, and a relaxed attitude creates fun. I was having fun.

I arrived downstream at Calico Bluffs about 7:30 pm, unloaded the canoe, and set up camp.

———————

INTO THE COUNTRY

One of the first books I read after arriving in Alaska in 1978 was John McPhee's *Coming into the Country*. At the top of the cover of the paperback it read, "A voyage of spirit and mind into America's last great wilderness—Alaska." Those few words were spot on in their description. I carried the same old copy with me on my canoe trip in 2019 and read it again for the first time in 40 years. I reacted somewhat different to the stories this time—I had since met some of the people McPhee wrote about, and had visited many of the same places. The tales were no longer distant thoughts and ideas but a part of history that I had joined, at least in a small way. The theme, however, had not changed for me. It still was a story about Alaska and its people, and wild places, and how peoples' values shape everyday living. It was a story about how those values change, not so much for individuals, but for societies. In protecting Alaska's wild treasures for future generations, and with strong support by America as a whole at the time, the freedom cherished by many locals for many decades (to build cabins in the wilderness, mine gold without much regulation, and to take fish and wildlife for food without consideration of season or other restrictions) would be lost in short order. The passage of the Alaska National Interest Lands Conservation Act (referred by most simply as "ANILCA") in late 1980, soon spawned new regulations. The rulemakings were democratic and legal, and arguably for the greater good, but nonetheless, the last vestiges of American freedom to live off the land, largely as one pleased, and without much government interference, were lost. Some compromises were made in the legislation, and limited re-direction occurred over time through litigation, but for the most part, it can probably be agreed that ANILCA changed Alaska forever. While I personally supported the conservation provisions and the Act's overall objectives, I too could not help but mourn the loss of simpler times and the freedom they held.

For those who have read McPhee's book you know that "The Country" that he referred to is the Upper Yukon River region, and at the time of the book's writing, the area was being proposed to be set aside as a national monument. Indeed, with the passage of ANILCA, the entire drainage of the Charley River and 115 miles of the Yukon River and surrounding uplands were re-designated from general lands (held by the Bureau of Land Management) to the new Yukon–Charley Rivers National Preserve managed by the National Park Service.

As I reached the terminus of the Taylor Highway at the town of Eagle in July 1979. I recall a large wooden sign that read, "Don't Let the Park Service Into the Country." It didn't take a mind reader to know how the locals felt about the federal government then. In the time I spent in Alaska leading up to the passing of ANILCA, and for a half a dozen years or so after, the animosity exhibited in some places toward federal employees was plain to see and sometimes bordering on the threatening. It was not uncommon to be refused service at some gas stations in Interior Alaska when driving a government vehicle, so one needed to carry enough gasoline for at least one refilling. Once, while in uniform, I was even refused service when trying to order a milkshake at a Tasty Freeze. More disturbing, however, were the times I was physically threatened. Many folks were mad, really mad, and sometimes fueled by a little alcohol and/or peer pressure, things could get a little dicey. No matter that I, or practically any federal employee in Alaska at the time, had nothing to do with the setting aside of millions of acres of Alaska lands for conservation purposes; Washington, D.C. was a long ways away and we were handy. Ultimately no harm ever came to me from any of the threats and they did subside as I got older and as the passage of ANILCA faded in the rearview mirror.

———————————

I looked at the gigantic striations in the mountains across the river from my camp. Such geologic wonders are prominent in the Upper Yukon region. They provide outstanding nesting habitat for peregrine falcons and other raptors which are numerous, and their sightings offer reward to the boater, who doesn't have to pay super-careful attention to the water ahead in this section of the river. The birds are just the icing on the cake though, as the bluffs themselves are awe-inspiring. What is most striking is that the striations, deposited over millennia, are near vertical rather than horizontal. Over time these gigantic mounds have been lifted up and turned on their side.

Yukon is said to mean "Great River" so named by the Gwich'in people who have lived in the region for thousands of years. It certainly is a great river, being the third longest in North America. It originates from the glacier-fed Atlin Lake in British Columbia and flows 715 miles through B.C. and Yukon territories before entering Alaska, and then flowing another 1,267 miles to its mouth at the Yukon–Kuskokwim Delta and the Bering Sea. After retirement I drafted a standard bucket list of places to see and things to do, and this included a 1,000-mile canoe trip on the Yukon River. I softened the 1,000 mile goal a bit later, wanting neither the hassles of the international crossing by starting in Canada nor the frequent delays that can occur waiting out weather on the lower river. Practicality entered the equation too. While one can charter a float plane pickup along much of the river, or fly out from numerous villages along the way, there are only three road-accessible points (that you can drive to) in Alaska: Eagle, at the terminus of the Taylor Highway, Circle, at the terminus of the Steese Highway, and the Yukon Crossing on the Dalton Highway (in route to Prudhoe Bay). I felt the distance from Eagle to Circle was too short (158 miles) and too easy (with a current of often over 5 miles per hours and a route that was easy to navigate) and so opted to go to "the bridge." This would be a 408-mile trip from Eagle and should take only a couple of weeks.

The daily routine on a solo trip is whatever you make of it. All decisions are yours to make: when you start and finish the day, when and what you eat, where you camp, and whatever side trips you may want to make to explore interesting areas. It is a great stress reducer to be in control of the basic elements of your day. If you are tired, take a nap, if you are hungry, eat a snack, if you are unclean, go for a swim. Another postretirement bucket list item for me was to backpack the Oregon section of the Pacific Crest Trail; on completion I found that I liked the independence of going at my own pace and altering my routine for whatever whim struck me. For that trip, my wife Shannon re-supplied me at three highway crossings during my month-long hike so I didn't have to carry all my food for the 500+ miles. I hiked as little as 12 miles a day and as much as 23. The canoe trip on the Yukon was similar, in that I largely set the pace of travel but was also different in two ways. First, when hiking you can "go" rain or shine, but when paddling solo, if the wind comes up from an unfavorable direction, it can be fruitless, or even dangerous, to continue. Second, and on the bright side, using a canoe allows you to take a lot more snacks, books, and other goodies than when everything has to fit in a bag on your back. I like goodies.

Though I had ample room in the canoe, I still opted largely for freeze-dried food for dinners. I supplemented that with cheese or peanut butter and crackers, Hershey's Kisses, and a little red wine. Breakfast generally included coffee, oatmeal, dried fruit, and a granola bar. Lunch is non-existent for me, whether hiking or paddling. I snack throughout the day eating nuts, raisins, jerky, energy bars, trail mix, and an occasional candy bar. Food was stowed in a large waterproof bag, except what I kept out for the day's snacking. The bag was tied to the crossbeams of the canoe during the day and hung on a tree when possible at night. My stove, fuel, and cooking gear were stowed in a small cooler and lashed into the mid-section of the canoe to provide a bit more stability and support. Another waterproof duffle contained my sleeping bag, pad, and extra clothes. A final duffle contained my tent, tarp, extra rope, and a folding stool. A fishing rod, an extra paddle, and a 12-gauge shotgun were lashed in where easy to reach. My water jug was in the bow—its weight useful to countermine (near the stern). Finally, I had an emergency floatation bag tethered to my life jacket that included maps, a Garmin InReach (emergency satellite location beacon/GPS), waterproof matches and fire starter, extra ammunition, a camera, first aid supplies, some high-energy food, stocking cap and gloves, a light-weight rain jacket, and a small air horn. I also wore a small fanny pack at all times that contained a knife, insect repellant, head net, cigarette lighter, space blanket, collapsible cup, water purification tablets, and a SPOT (emergency satellite communication device).

While my return to The Country was more a planned trip down memory lane than an effort to experience some new adventure in Alaska's wilds, other people are drawn from around the world to the area for that very reason. Wilderness is a fleeting resource. I use the term generally, for in the United States, there is congressionally designated wilderness, protected by the Wilderness Act of 1964, and other wild places that have wilderness qualities and values but are not legally protected for those specific values. When speaking of such things, many land managers refer to designated wilderness as "Big W" Wilderness, and other wild and remote areas, but not congressionally designated, as "Little w" wilderness. Alaska has plenty of both, and many wild areas not specifically included in the National Wilderness System in Alaska have other protections. Still, different purposes and exceptions allow for some erosion of wilderness qualities over time in most areas not protected by the Wilderness Act. This truth is not meant to cause alarm. In and of itself it is not a bad thing. Different factions will always debate whether we should have more or less "Big W" Wilderness, but I would argue that wilderness, no matter how defined, is of such tremendous value that it would irreparably harm both humans and wild creatures if it is lost, and once lost, it would be near impossible to restore. The Country is "Little w" wilderness, but it is wild. People are drawn to it because it is undeveloped, rugged, sparsely populated, scenic, isolated, and peaceful. I have been fortunate enough to hike to the Incan ruins of Machu Picchu in Peru, swim in the Lena River in Yakutia, Russia, and be covered by the mist from Victoria Falls in Zambia. I have also been fortunate enough to see wild tigers in the foothills of the Himalayas in India, polar bears waiting the freeze-up of Hudson Bay in Manitoba, and a kiwi calling to a mate on the remote Stewart Island in New Zealand. These and many other experiences are wonderful, but to sit by yourself many miles from the nearest human, under the light of the midnight sun, listening to the distant cry of a loon, and watching a wolf trot along the banks of the Yukon River—that is, well, beyond words. It's an experience, a feeling. It is something that that requires effort to experience and yet requires nothing really at all, except time and place, and that place must be wilderness.

Pre-ANILCA sentiments – Eagle, Alaska.

Upper Yukon River – 1979.

Upper Yukon River – 2019.

Chapter Two:

IN THE BEGINNING

I awoke on the third morning and peered out of the tent to see slight movement on a muddy peninsula in the distance. A young lynx was slowly walking toward the water where several families of Canada geese loafed. The birds had grazed the new grass to fine nubs and there was no cover between them and the cat. It had zero chance of getting a goose for breakfast—still it apparently had nothing better to do than try. At about 100 meters out, the geese moved off and the lynx walked slowly back the way it had come and disappeared into the high willows along the river bank. I watched the scene unfold and thought briefly about all of the wonders that were occurring across the huge expanse of Alaska at that very moment and how most were not witnessed by any human. Alaska is so big. Its coastline is 33,000 nautical miles along. From the tip of the Aleutian Islands east to the tip of the Alaskan Panhandle is approximately 2,300 miles. When I first moved to Alaska it had five time zones (there are only two now and unless you travel to Adak in the Aleutians, there is only one that matters). It has few roads and a population density of about one person per square mile. In comparison, Wyoming has about six.

What one observes of the Alaskan landscape today is the result of countless years of glaciation, volcanic activity, uplifting from earthquakes, wind storms, and the annual potential of nearly 200 degrees Fahrenheit temperature fluctuations. It is a land of extremes. The fish and wildlife living in Alaska are well adapted to the unique habitats found there. The wood frog (only amphibian or reptile found naturally through most of the state) can over-winter by burying in mud that freezes. The Arctic grayling feeds voraciously in the thaw months and then lies dormant in the long, dark winter, often in water which may register zero dissolved oxygen levels under a thick layer of ice. The great brown bear, also well adapted, will gain hundreds of pounds by eating protein-rich salmon in the fall before hibernating for months in a small earthen den (and gradually losing hundreds of pounds during "sleep").

The Indigenous people that inhabited Alaska prior to Russian colonization and European influence from fur trappers, whalers, and gold miners, were no less well adapted to survive in Alaska's harsh environment. They did so with only limited natural objects for clothing, shelter, heat and light generation, transportation, weapons, and food and its preservation. No nylon, Gortex, canvas, rubber, steel, batteries, rifles, camp stoves, or compasses—and even more amazing to me, they survived without DEET to repel the inevitable hordes of mosquitoes that arrive early every summer, and without matches or lighters or anything dependable to start a fire. I have visited the remains of ancient sod huts overlooking the Arctic Ocean and cannot help but be filled with respect and admiration. Those areas are devoid of trees, are snow- and ice-covered longer than not every year, the availability of most fish and wildlife is severely limited, and during the long, cold winter, the inhabitants go many days without the sun ever rising above the horizon. People lived there and not only survived, but raised families and have passed on a rich cultural heritage over many thousands of years.

Alaska has a unique and rich natural history, and there are many stories that could be shared about its "beginnings"—or earlier times, including its prehistory when much of the region was believed to be a great deal warmer and inhabited by creatures such as camels and saber-toothed cats, or the extended period of human migration to the new world across the Bering Land Bridge, or the rich and diverse Native cultures existing prior to European contact. There are more modern "beginnings" too, including

Alaska's purchase from Russia and its path to statehood. This is the part of Alaska's history that I want to share briefly, for it is largely that which created the working environment that drew me to Alaska in the first place and kept me there for 30 years. This, in essence, is its conservation history—the awareness of the unique value of its wildlife and wild places, and efforts to protect them.

Alaska Purchase, 1867.

Apparently Russia feared it might lose the Alaska territory it held without any payment (most likely to the British) and probably had exploited its resources as far as they reasonably could foresee any sustained use (primarily in sea otter pelts) and therefore sought to unload the faraway, and likely difficult to defend, place. Negotiations concluded with the United States on March 30, 1867, and a signed treaty resulted in the transfer of 586,412 square miles for the price of $7,200,000 (less than two cents per acre). Even at that price some Americans scoffed at the deal and labelled it "Seward's Folly" (after Secretary of State William Seward), "Seward's Icebox," "Walrussia," or "Icebergia." Gold was yet undiscovered and the timber and salmon resources were probably generally known but not commercially viable to exploit due to lack of reasonable infrastructure and transportation at such a great distance from the contiguous United States. Furs, however, could be easily transported by a sailing ship, and efforts to harvest sea otters and fur seals dominated the earliest efforts to benefit economically from the new acquisition. Commercial whaling soon followed and then large salmon canneries, mining operations, and "adventuring," the latter to include early scientific explorations and notable efforts (in time and travel) in pursuit of unique big-game hunting opportunities.

A combination of early visitors to the Alaska territory sparked the earliest efforts to conserve its resources and protect some of its lands. George B. Grinnell (1849–1938), Madison Grant (1865–1937), William T. Hornaday

(1854–1937), and Charles A. Sheldon (1867–1928), all active members in the Boone and Crockett Club, had great influence in the establishment of game laws and game preserves in the new territory and in the protection of some of its greatest treasures, like Mt. McKinley Denali National Park and Preserve—established in 1917 (a particular effort by Sheldon). Men like Henry W. Elliot (1846–1930) worked to save the northern fur seal from over-exploitation and possible extinction. William H. Dall (1845–1927) made 14 or more trips to Alaska while working for the U.S. Coast Survey and U.S. Geological Survey as an explorer, writer, and scientist and became a significant conservation advocate. John Muir (1838–1914) also made at least seven trips to Alaska between 1879 and 1899. Muir believed nature had a spiritual power and should be protected. He once paraphrased Henry David Thoreau in a field notebook entry in writing, "IN GOD'S WILDNESS LIES THE HOPE OF THE WORLD…." Harvard-educated Thoreau (1817–1862) influenced many besides Muir. He was a philosopher and author who argued for truth, justice, and living in a natural world with simplicity. His insights are timeless. My favorite Thoreau quote, and one I tried to take to heart in later years as a government manager and administrator, is that "the government is best which governs the least." The advice, while always sound, can create a paradox at times as the government is challenged to conserve natural resources for the sustained use of people and also protect the integrity of the natural environment, knowing the wild creatures cannot argue their own case.

Early visitors to the Alaskan territory were immediately struck by its vastness and beauty. Some were also participants in an age of awakening during which conservation was at the forefront. They had witnessed the plight of the plains' bison and passenger pigeon. Those with conviction and a willingness to share their passion, created a foundation of interest in protecting part of Alaska's natural wonders that was easy for those who followed to take up. Early leaders of the Bureau of Biological Survey including C. Hart Merriam (1855–1942), Edward W. Nelson (1855–1934), and Iran N. Gabrielson (1889–1977) are a few of such people who took special interest in Alaska and worked to provide conservation-minded direction and protection. Early game laws and the establishment of early preserves were the result.

Statehood 1959.

Between 1879 and 1884, the United States Navy had governing responsibilities for Alaska. In 1884, new legislation created a civil and judicial district that provided the territory with marshals and judges. Following the 1897–1898 Klondike Gold Rush, and the resulting significant increase in the human population in the north, additional legislation (1900) created an official code of civil and criminal process, and a means to collect taxes. In 1912, Congress officially made Alaska a territory and provided for a legislature to be elected (to include eight senators and 16 members of a house of representatives). In this action, however, Congress still reserved the right to manage Alaska's natural resources.

The first attempt to make Alaska a state came in 1916 when the population of the territory was believed to be less than 60,000. The bill, introduced by James Wickersham (elected delegate to Congress), failed due to lack of interest. National political attention in Alaska largely focused on its fishery resources and copper mining until the war years. By 1943, over half of Alaska's estimated 233,000 people were affiliated with the military. Alaska was at the forefront for a significant amount of war effort and was regularly in the news—Japanese forces had occupied U.S. soil on two of the Aleutian Islands, and Alaska was critical in facilitating the Lend–Lease Act provisions that supplied Russia with critical materials to aid in the fight against Germany. The Alaska Highway, approximately 1,600 miles long, was constructed by about 11,000 soldiers in just eight months. Alaska was then connected to the "Lower 48" via a road through Canada. After the war many veterans stayed in Alaska and more people came to visit. The population grew and so did the desire of many for statehood. A 1946 referendum supporting statehood led to the creation of the Alaska Statehood Association, and in 1949, the Alaska Statehood Commission was formed. A bill to make Alaska the 49th state passed the House by 186 to 146 in 1950 but did not pass in the Senate. The major concern seemed to be worry that the new state majority would vote Democrat and threaten the slim Republican majority in Congress at the time.

Dedicated Alaskans worked hard to get their statehood ambitions furthered via multiple efforts. In 1956 they elected Ernest Gruening and William Eagan as Senators-elect and Ralph Rivers as (House) Representative-elect, but these men were not officially included or recognized by Congress. They did continue to lobby hard for their cause, however, along with Bob Bartlett (official Delegate), and in 1958, President Eisenhower endorsed the Alaska statehood proposal. Some continued debate occurred and amendments were proposed, including one to retain federal control of fish and game until the Secretary of Interior determined that the state could meet necessary conservation provisions and ensure continued nonresident access. On January 3, 1959, Alaska was officially declared the 49th state and the new flag would have seven rows of seven stars (for a short time, Hawaii became the 50th state on August 21 of the same year).

Alaska statehood would result in drastic changes in how people would live and work in the far north. Perhaps the most important factor in the changes was with the land itself. The first legislation for statehood provided that Alaska would get 15 to 20 million acres of land based upon the quantification of the old public lands concept that granted two sections, 16 and 36, of every township to a western state. Congress discussed this at some length however and decided that in order for the new state to survive economically it needed a large resource base. Ultimately the Statehood Act granted title to the new state 104 million acres of land to be selected from that not already specifically reserved by the federal government (national parks, wildlife refuges, national forests, and military reservations). This was far more land than had ever been granted to any other new state, but with all of Alaska being approximately 375 million acres, it still was only about 28 percent of the state. This guaranteed a large continuing federal presence and set the stage for a variety of conflicts, primarily over management of natural resources.

ANCSA 1971.

With the new state starting to select lands from the vast federal domain in Alaska the issue of Native land entitlements began to get serious attention. In both the agreement transferring Alaska from Russia to the United States, and in the Statehood Act, discussions occurred on the rights of Native Alaskans. Most agreed that rights exists but that they were not defined and would have to be resolved in future legislation or litigation. When one thinks about it, Alaska Natives were somewhat unique in the history of our Nation. They had unarguably lived on the land, possessing it, for thousands of years and unlike many Lower 48 tribes, they had not been subdued in battle or been signatories to treaties. Now the land they had lived on for generations was being divided and there was no clear resolution to the matter of Native claims. Secretary of Interior, Udall, put a freeze on state selections in 1966 and at that time title had only transferred to about 12 million acres. The accepted primary impetus for resolution of Native claims, however, was the discovery of oil at Prudhoe Bay that would require a pipeline to an ice-free port (ultimately constructed over approximately 800 miles from the Beaufort Sea to Valdez). Land claim challenges could conceivably hold up permits and related construction decisions for many years. On December 18, 1971, Congress passed the Alaska Native Claims Settlement Act (ANCSA). The law extinguished any rights to lands and their resources that might be claimed by Alaska Natives. In exchange, 12 "for profit" regional corporations were formed (with a 13th added later to represent interests of Alaska Natives who did not reside in the state), along with over 200 village corporations, and giving these entities 44 million acres of federal lands and $962.5 million.

While ANCSA was a monumental achievement supported by many, some Alaskan Natives were shocked with the deal and argued it would accelerate the loss of Native culture, and that the decisions made by a small group of leaders unfairly committed all Native people for all time. Nonetheless, Alaska's federal lands were being divided, and as discussions continued on what lands state and Native interests would select (generally based on presumed value—often the potential for oil and gas, minerals, or timber), other discussions were underway as to what Alaska lands, remaining under federal control, should be set aside for conservation.

ANILCA 1980.

Section 17(d)(2) of ANCSA granted the ability for the Secretary of Interior to withdraw up to 80 million acres of land (over a two-year period) to be studied for possible inclusion in the National Park, National Wildlife Refuge, National Wild and Scenic Rivers, or National Forest Systems. One day before the two years ran out, "d-2" study recommendations were submitted to Congress as legislative proposals which also put in place a five-year deadline, and if not met the proposals would die for lack of action. The five years would expire December 17, 1978. The 95th Congress adjourned in October of 1978 without enacting the proposed legislation, although the House had passed it earlier in May by a vote of 277 to 31. On November 16, 1978, the Secretary of Interior (Cecil Andrus) used authority under the Federal Land Policy and Management Act (FLPMA) to withdraw 105 million acres of Alaska land for approximately three years. The Secretary of Agriculture withdrew another 11 million acres for approximately two years. On December 1, 1978, President Carter used the Antiquities Act of 1906 to withdraw over 55 million acres of federal lands in Alaska and designated them national monuments to be managed by the National Park Service, U.S. Fish and Wildlife Service (FWS), or U.S. Forest Service. The Secretary of Interior then again used FLPMA to withdraw 40 million acres (February 12, 1980) to complement the President's withdrawals and extend the deadline for earlier actions. The withdrawals made it clear that the federal government was serious about protecting some of its holdings in Alaska for conservation purposes and forced compromise from political factions that either thought such protections were ill advised for future economic development needs or were too extensive and should be scaled back. Congressman Don Young in 1977 testified (in a subcommittee hearing as part of the House Committee on Interior and Insular Affairs) that, "Alaska is more than environmental treasure, it is a resource storehouse. Alaska is also environmentally important. It is a vast land with many unique and unparalleled scenic and wildlife values. No one denies this nor the need to protect such values. Disagreements stem from how much land must be set aside to preserve these unique areas."

In the end, the Alaska National Interest Lands Conservation Act (ANILCA) was signed into law on December 2, 1980. The Act terminated all earlier withdrawals and set aside 104.3 million acres, creating 25 national wild and scenic rivers; 12 new national parks, monuments, and preserves; 11 new national wildlife refuges; and the Steese National Conservation Area and White Mountains National Recreation Area (managed by the Bureau of Land Management). It also added 12.3 million acres to preexisting parks, refuges, and national forests, and designated more than 52 million acres of the conservation lands as wilderness.

This brief summary of ANILCA only brushes the surface of the politics and debate that took place in its passage. Many Alaskans felt betrayed—lands in their backyard were being "locked up." Conservationists nation-wide were generally pleased but recognized that ANILCA contained many compromises and didn't protect all that they had hoped for. Provisions that allowed continued use of snow machines, motorboats, and airplanes in newly designated Wilderness bothered some. The carving out of some areas for future resource development was also annoying for many. Some areas were given special attention to allow for development immediately and others left the door open for future study and decision. A classic example of this was for the Coastal Plain of the Arctic National Wildlife Refuge (ANILCA Section 1002) where Congress reserved a future decision to themselves as to whether to open the area for oil and gas development. Eventually they did authorize leasing in the Refuge (as part of the 2017 Tax Bill) but to date no on-the-ground activity has commenced.

During my time in Alaska, I had the opportunity to meet President Carter on two occasions. Both times he spoke about Alaska lands conser-vation and mentioned that during his presidency he has vivid memory of three maps: the American Embassy in Iran, the Panama Canal Zone, and the proposed conservation lands in Alaska. Although many people and organizations made it happen, without the President's interest and support it is unlikely that the landmark conservation action that ANILCA represents would have transpired. And whether people look fondly to the Act, or grimace at its mention, I know too that my life was indirectly changed forever by its passage. With all the new responsibilities in Alaska following the passage of ANILCA came the designation of a new U.S. Fish and Wildlife Service (FWS) region, new funding and mandates, and a great deal of opportunity for a fledgling biologist.

My career in Alaska began in October 1978 where I held a temporary position as a staff writer/photographer for the FWS in Anchorage, Alaska. This assignment was fortuitous for it allowed me to travel about the state and report on special projects and field operations, meeting people and learning about the vastness and diversity of the land. I then held several other temporary jobs working on contaminants issues, subsistence take of walrus, and developing a report on the most environmentally friendly route for a proposed natural gas pipeline. I also worked for the Alaska Department of Fish and Game on sportfish projects near Yakutat and as a deckhand on a halibut long-liner out of Seward. I was content to stay in Alaska, but an upcoming hiring freeze announced by the new Reagan Administration had me scramble to find permanent status with FWS. I took the first job I was offered and it happened to be a GS-5 Biological Technician Position in Yazoo City, Mississippi. Leaving most my belongings with friends in Alaska, I flew south and worked with alligators and wood ducks (among other critters) for six months, gaining "permanent status," though still under probation and looking for a way back to Alaska.

In May of 1981, I returned north as a Fish and Wildlife Biologist, GS-7/9/11, working in Fairbanks on contaminants' issues. I was married to Shannon in November that year and we soon settled in a one-room cabin about 15 miles out of town. We had no plumbing, so I hauled water daily for our sled dogs and us. It was a simple life, and somewhat harsh, but we accumulated many fond memories of our time in the cabin. While in Fairbanks, I changed jobs twice. I became a Fisheries Biologist (GS-11) in April of 1984 and spent several years working on baseline studies of fishes on refuges in Northern Alaska. Most of the effort was focused on the 1002 area of the Arctic National Wildlife Refuge conducting studies mandated by Congress. In May of 1987, I became the Assistant Refuge Manager for the Yukon Flats National Wildlife Refuge (GS-11). During this time I spent a couple months in Georgia being trained as a dual-function law enforcement officer. In September 1988, expecting our first child, Shannon and I moved to Cold Bay where I became the Refuge Manager of Izembek National Wildlife Refuge (GS-12). This unique assignment also created many strong memories, and we had our three children while stationed there. Because of the Refuge's remoteness and lack of medical facilities, having three little ones changed our view of life and we sought to move closer to town (Cold Bay is approximately 650 miles by air to Anchorage). In March of 1991, I became the Regional Migratory Bird Coordinator (Wildlife Biologist, GS-13) for the Alaska Region of FWS. While stationed in Anchorage, this position required extensive travel, primarily to rural villages and to Washington, D.C. In October 1995, I became the Refuge Manager of Kenai National Wildlife Refuge and moved the family to Soldotna where we stayed for 14 years. From there, with the kids all situated in college, Shannon and I left Alaska for Portland, Oregon, where I finished my career with FWS, first as a Refuge Supervisor and finally as the Regional Chief of Refuges (Fish and Wildlife Administrator, GS-15). In my last position, I had administrative responsibilities for over 75 national wildlife refuges located in Oregon, Washington, Idaho, Hawaii, part of Nevada, and the remote Pacific Islands (including refuges in Guam, American Samoa, and the Commonwealth of the Northern Mariana Islands).

Thirty-five years as a biologist, manager, and administrator with FWS went pretty fast. Time seems to pass rapidly when one is busy and I always had plenty to do. In retirement I stay busy too and one of my passions is to revisit places where I have worked or played previously—places like The Country—the Upper Yukon River. While many return visits to previous haunts show dramatic change (the house I grew up in near Grants Pass, Oregon, has been replaced with a Sonic Burger, and the adjacent fields I once roamed are now a shopping mall) some remain largely unchanged. The Upper Yukon is largely unchanged, safe for now, and that seems to me a good thing—a very good thing.

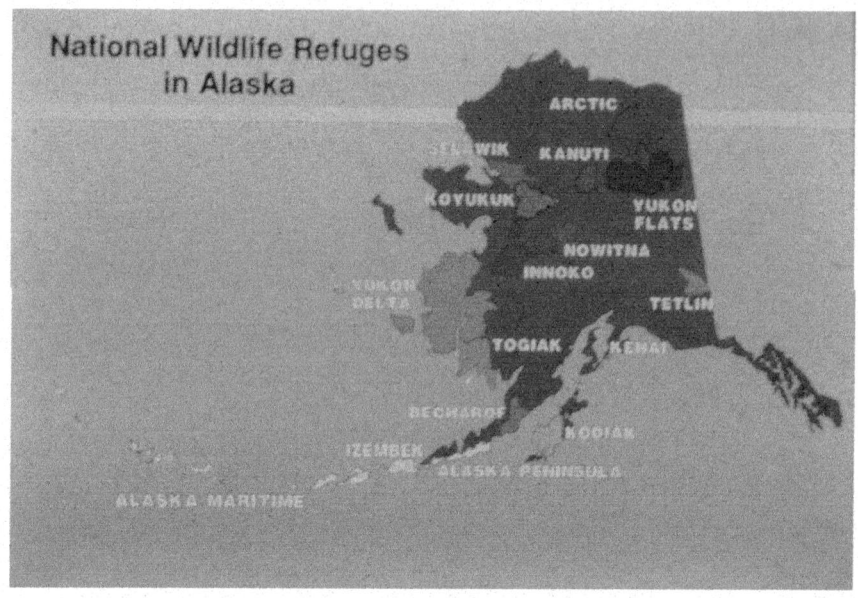

Post ANILCA National Wildlife Refuges in Alaska.

President Carter kept a strong interest in Alaska after ANILCA.

Chapter Three:
WATER WATER EVERYWHERE

As I looked out at the sweeping expanse of river ahead, I was reminded what had brought me to The Country in the first place. I was working as a temporary employee for the FWS stationed out of the area office in Anchorage, Alaska. Oversight for the area office came from the regional headquarters in Portland, Oregon. Alaska became its own region a short time later—shortly after the passage of ANILCA (largely due to the responsibility to administer millions of new acres added to the National Wildlife Refuge System). For all practical purposes, however, Alaska was managed largely with autonomy in the early days too, due to its unique resources and challenges, and the long distance to Portland.

During my first visit to The Country four decades previous, I was working with the Environmental Contaminants Evaluation (ECE) branch of the Habitat Preservation Program for FWS. The work focused on monitoring potential impacts to fish and wildlife from environmental pollutants on federal lands or impacts that could stem from federally permitted projects. The work examined the effects of placer mining on anadromous fish streams, the impacts of sulfite waste liquor discharged from pulp mills in Southeast Alaska, the effects of agricultural chemicals used in the Delta Barley Project, the reason for waterfowl die-offs associated with a military training activities, oil and gas reserve pit and pipeline safety issues, and a whole host of other projects. The work on the Upper Yukon River was focused on asbestos in the water and its potential impacts to the health of fish and wildlife in the area.

How we were first set upon this issue as a potential concern I do not know, but water samples collected from the Yukon in 1977 showed in excess of a billion asbestos fibers per liter of water. The sampling of fish and wildlife that started in 1979, and continued through 1982, resulted in asbestos being found in everything that we looked at. Tissue samples from muscle and/or internal organs were sent to the Lake Superior Basin Study Center (University of Minnesota at Duluth) where slides were prepared and carefully examined under an electron microscope. Both amphibole and chrysotile fibers (the second type considered more dangerous because it is finer and sharper) were found in resident fish (burbot, northern pike, Arctic grayling, round whitefish, and long-nosed sucker), migrating fish (king salmon and sheefish), a migratory bird (solitary sandpiper), resident bird (raven), and resident mammals (black bear and beaver). The study results probably raised more questions than answers. Asbestos is of a health concern, but it was a naturally occurring mineral fiber. And now that we knew it penetrated and lodged in tissues of basically anything that ingested Yukon River water, what could anyone do about it?

And so, when I returned to The Country after many years, I had the asbestos project results embedded in my gray matter—esoteric information to some perhaps, but clearly on my mind nonetheless. In Samuel Taylor Coleridge's *The Rime of the Ancient Mariner*, he wrote, "Water, water everywhere, nor any drop to drink"—referring to a sailor surrounded by an ocean of undrinkable saltwater. Knowing what I did about the Yukon River's mineral content, I felt the same way and was compelled to seek my drinking water from other sources than the main stem of the Yukon. It was almost certainly unnecessary paranoia—local people have drank directly from the river for generations and science suggests that if any problem to human health related to asbestos is to occur, it will likely be decades in the making. (And at my age why should I concern myself?) I had options though, so I used them. In the upper reaches it was not difficult to paddle close to shore and fill water jugs when coming upon a freshwater tributary. Downstream, into the Yukon Flats and beyond, such a process is easier said than done. The river braids, broadens, and slows. Muddy oxbows encircle islands, and finding any freshwater source can become an effort in futility. In these situations I looked for nearshore fresher mixing zones (downstream of a major clear water tributary), filled all containers for maximum storage (so as not to have to repeat too often), and then filtered the water before use.

The asbestos study was a bit of an anomaly, and most of the contaminants studies we completed did not result in questioning looks from managers and industry leaders that the Upper Yukon work undoubtedly did. From the mid-1970s to the mid-1990s, scientific knowledge about the effects of a variety of pollutants increased rapidly, and rules to restrict use followed close behind. I remember when growing up in the 1960s how I could buy elemental mercury at the pharmacy and roll it around playfully in the palm of my hand. I would buy formaldehyde in the same store, and use it to preserve frogs and snakes in Mason jars and display them on shelves in my cluttered bedroom. Like asbestos, the dangers just weren't known at the time. Soon though, lead would be removed from paint, gasoline, and shotgun ammunition that we used to hunt waterfowl. DDT and other pesticides would be banned. Industrial use of chromium, zinc, and other heavy metals would be regulated.

One chemical compound, polychlorinated biphenyls (PCBs), wasn't found to be a risk and regulated until too late to have prevented environmental harm at Kenai National Wildlife Refuge in southcentral Alaska. The ECE Branch of FWS was conducting a National Environmental Pollutant Monitoring Program to look at concentrations and trends of environmental contaminants in fish and wildlife nationwide. Two common species were collected in most parts of the United States—starlings and rainbow trout. To my knowledge no starlings were in Alaska in the 1970s and 1980s (though I have seen some recently in Anchorage), but rainbow trout were available throughout most of southern Alaska. The Swanson River was the site chosen to collect the fish as it was accessible from Anchorage and had a history of providing brood stock for a pre-statehood federal hatchery. Swanson River also flows through the Kenai National Wildlife Refuge and the Swanson River Oil Field. Results of the testing caused a bit of a surprise nationally. Alaska was believed to be largely pristine and the fish showed small amounts of some pesticides and heavy metals, but also noticeably elevated levels of PCBs. A little sleuthing quickly determined the source. An explosion at the compressor plant in the oilfield in January of 1972 released large amounts of the oily liquid, and since it wasn't yet regulated, the State permitted its disposal along the oilfield gravel roads to help with dust control. Years later, after extensive excavation of soils, incineration, and disposal—costing over $40 million—the problem was largely ameliorated.

A few years later, when I was stationed in the Fairbanks Field Office as the first federal fish and wildlife contaminants biologist in Alaska, I worked extensively on oilfield issues in and around Prudhoe Bay. Of concern were practices associated with reserve pits on drilling pads. Drill muds, laced with heavy metals and often lubricated with hydrocarbons, were used to aid the drilling process and the muds and cuttings were collected in pits on gravel pads at the drill site. Snow removal during the long, dark winter usually entailed plowing snow from the access roads and pads to the side and/or into the pits. With melting in the spring, the pits would begin to overflow and were managed by pumping contaminated water over the pit berm to the adjacent tundra areas, or pumping into tankers and then sprayed on gravel roads (like at Kenai, with a State-issued permit to address dust control). Concerns over the effects on the area's tundra wetlands, the macroinvertebrates that lived there, and ultimately the migratory birds that used the inverts for food were valid. Fieldwork started in 1983 and published (Fish and Wildlife Service) Biological Report 87(7) in 1987, concluded that a significant correlation existed between contaminated reserve pits and the abundance and diversity of macroinvertebrates. Industry soon began to make changes that eliminated additives that contained chromium and other heavy metals, switched from oil-based to water-based muds, and then also to grind and inject the muds and cuttings back down the hole. By 1994 zero discharge of all waste fluids was realized and eventually old pits were closed and much of the stored waste was removed and properly disposed.

Another issue I worked on in the early years was placer mining. The practice had been undertaken for nearly a century in Alaska and had made a few people very rich, and provided "living money" for a whole lot of other folks who tried to eke out a living the best they could from the land. While some gold-mining operations might entail the use of cyanide or mercury to collect fine gold, most placer mining operations simply tried to recover larger flakes or nuggets from sluicing operations. All things being equal, they made more money by the more dirt they moved. Their sin was in muddying the water—legal standards were set for settable solids and turbidity, both for human use and (at different levels) for the protection of fish and wild-life—and most of the larger placer operations far exceeded the set standards. Initially I reviewed all federal permits being issued for placer mining in the State. These were "NPDES" permits issued by the Environmental Protection Agency (EPA) under Section 402 of the Clean Water Act (National Pollutant Discharge Elimination System permits for non-point source discharged into the waters of the United States). At the time the closest permanent EPA office was in Seattle, Washington, and the permit system was not very effective; some operators chose to ignore the permit requirement and compliance checks were rare for those who did get permits. The program transitioned to nationwide general permits and the workload dropped significantly. At the time I thought the EPA was either dropping the ball on enforcement or being super strategic in giving plenty of time for miners to transition to the new permits and conditions. Probably both were true, but phasing in the program changes was smart. It gave time for miners to talk among their peers and sort through a paradigm shift that almost certainly would have been much uglier if it had been forced quickly. For most operations, standards could be met by constructing settling ponds and most of the larger oper-ations already were using heavy equipment to move dirt. Like all changes that require additional time and effort, there were however some casualties to the industry either by not being able to afford the additional expense or just not wanting to deal with the bureaucracy and calling it quits.

One of the most colorful individuals I met during the placer mining debates was Joe Vogler. Joe had a reputation for being cranky but he was always polite when we spoke and seemed to have a good sense of humor and a strong opinion about government control and eroding freedoms. He would frequently come to public meetings in Fairbanks wearing a bolo tie and holding a copy of the Bible in one hand and the U.S. Constitution in the other. Joe founded the Alaska Independence Party, felt the vote for statehood had been illegal, and argued frequently for Alaska to secede from the Union. He also ran for governor unsuccessfully on multiple occasions and took on not just take the feds but also the local government and even neighbors (who failed to cut aspen trees on land he sold them under conditions that they remove the "arboreal weeds"). He was a character but one that made Alaska politics interesting. When he disappeared in 1993, rumors were rampant. Conspiracy theorists believed that the Park Service may have made him disappear, citing legal battles stemming from Joe being caught with a D-8 cat in the Yukon–Charley Rivers National Preserve (in 1984). Others blamed unknown government assassins, citing the fact that Joe was scheduled to speak to the United Nations about Alaskan Independence a few weeks after he disappeared (and that "the government" wouldn't like that). After 16 months of conspiracy stories though, Joe was found wrapped in a blue tarp in a shallow grave north of Fairbanks and his killer was soon apprehended, tried, and sentenced to 80 years. Joe's death was the result of a robbery gone bad. His final wishes were followed and he was buried in Canada (Dawson City, Yukon) "not under the American flag."

———

Contaminants' issues can generate a lot of public outcry. Fear is easily generated whether warranted or not. There will always be unknown effects on the environment when using human-manufactured chemical compounds. There is only so much that can be reasonably be tested. The challenge is managing risks appropriately so that technology can be used for good in an environment of uncertainty. This challenge largely became the mission of the EPA and they have risen to it admirably. Sadly the science and processes employed by decision-makers can become political targets as they have to navigate the fear factors and often significant economic consequences of the decisions. I remember once briefing a politician (whom I won't name) about potential concerns to migrating salmon from low-level industrial pollutants being discharge into an Alaskan river. I was citing a study that had found sulfite waste liquor from pulp mills could interfere with the smoltification process of outmigrating juvenile salmon. The ability to change their osmoregulatory function to survive the transition from fresh to salt water is critical, and the chemicals being released were messing that up. This information only alarmed the politico and I was informed no studies would be conducted if they could help it—it was best not to know ... I was shocked, and saddened.

I recall former Secretary of Defense Donald Rumsfeld's famous saying, "Reports that say that something hasn't happened are always interesting to me, because as we know, there are known knowns; there are things we know we know. We also know there are known unknowns; that is to say we know there are some things we do not know." Science should focus on understanding more about the things we know we don't know. When it comes to environmental pollutants, however, the scariest things are the things that we don't know that we don't know.

Over time FWS largely got out of the contaminants biology business. A few qualified experts still exist in the rank and file but FWS no longer has an ECE branch or a research branch (removed and given to U.S. Geological Survey during the Clinton Administration) and the EPA has been legally charged with and funded to keep up with environmental pollution issues, whereas FWS has not. While the EPA often gets accused of government overreach, the public should be very concerned about any politically motivated redirection that affects the EPA's mandates or funding. While imperfect, they are the organization that has the best chance of protecting us from ourselves.

Howard Metsker – Upper Yukon River, 1979.

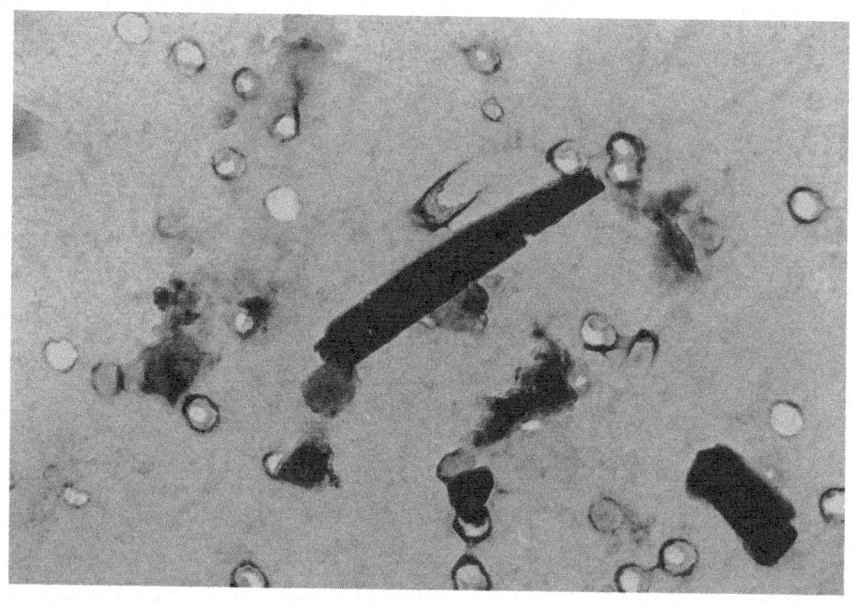

Asbestos fiber in northern pike muscle (magnified 10,000×).

Chapter Four:

CANOEING 101 (EIGHT LESSONS)

My Dad always told me while I was growing up that canoeing was just another way of swimming. I remember quizzing him frequently about getting a canoe when we portaged our rather heavy drift boat short distances to use the craft for duck hunting or lake fishing, or to reach a "secret spot" for steelhead fishing on the Rogue River near home. We never did acquire a canoe, and as I grew older, I appreciated Dad's wisdom more. I also grew to be more careful around flowing water in general after a near-death experience swimming in the Rogue River when on a boy scouting summer adventure. I learned that I was not as good a swimmer as I thought, or as good as many of the other boys in the troop. From then on I wore a lifejacket when using any small vessel on flowing water, and on more than one occasion, I tested their floatation properties. For the solo trip on the Upper Yukon River, I bought a three-person sport canoe and outfitted it with a homemade outrigger that prevented the boat from sinking and greatly reduced its ability to tip. That too got tested (and worked), perhaps therefore giving me the gift of future opportunities, and the ability to write this story.

My first Alaskan canoe experience came on July 4, 1979. My coworker, David Wiswar, and I rented a Coleman canoe, paddles, and lifejackets and drove to the upper reaches of Eagle River with the plan to paddle downstream to the Glenn Highway and hitch a ride with a yet to be determined person to take us back to our vehicle. Within a mile on the glacier-fed river we hit a sweeper and swamped the canoe (testing the rented lifejackets). We were soaked and cold. Though the day started sunny and warm, it grew overcast and the wind started coming up. Lesson one: bring a change of clothes in a dry bag and good fire-starting materials. As we shivered our way down to the highway, we started worrying about how long it might take to recruit a benevolent driver. This concern proved not to be unfounded (although eventually a young serviceman took pity on us). Lesson two: prepare for logistical contingencies and trip delays.

Another memorable Alaskan canoe experience occurred in June 1983. Fellow biologist Tony Booth and I struck out on a trip down Birch Creek near Circle, Alaska, planning to paddle approximately 130 miles from the Steese Highway near Eagle Summit, back to the highway crossing downstream. We were well-outfitted with a Grumman sport canoe and quality gear. Spring run-off was in full tilt and we made better time than expected. The upper reaches of Birch Creek were shallow and fast and there were many sharp bends. We started out scouting all of the blind corners downstream for obstacles and rapids before proceeding but soon got a little lazy about that. Approaching one such bend coming up downstream, Tony hollered to me, "Do you feel lucky?"

I think I said, "Yes." Moments later we rounded the bend and saw a large cottonwood tree across the stream and rapids rushing through it. We paddled hard for the left bank and made no noticeable progress, slamming into the tree, dipping the bow under the branches, and sinking the canoe. Tony had grabbed a branch from the bow and now stood midstream atop the fallen tree. Being in the stern as the canoe sank I went underwater with the boat and popped back up (due to wearing a float coat) having just enough time to grab and hang onto a large branch as the canoe disappeared downstream. I held on for a while, looking like a giant muskrat swimming upstream but making no progress, and contemplating my situation. If I let go I would be swept downstream and my hip boots were already full of water (and heavy enough I could not pull myself up onto the fallen tree). Would the float coat keep me up, or would the hip boots drag me down? I didn't want to find out. As I tired, the only other option seemed to be to kick off the hips boots and float away from the sweeper, but I had seen the canoe disappear with all of our gear into a frenzy of muddy water downstream and the thought of walking nearly 30 miles back up to the highway without any foot gear was also unappealing. Fortunately a third option played out. While I didn't have enough strength to pull myself up out of the water, the buoyancy allowed me to kind of float along and grab branches, like crossing monkey bars, until I reached an eddy and could pull myself up out of the slack water onto the tree trunk.

As Tony and I assessed our situation we knew we weren't to be picked up for over a week and had no means of communicating our predicament. We would have to either walk back to the highway without our camping gear or venture along the shore downstream and hope to recover the canoe and enough gear to complete the trip. We had lost our tent, sleeping bags, food, shotgun, and much more, but Tony did have a .44 magnum revolver in a shoulder holster, and I had been wearing a fanny pack that contained a fire starter, jerky and other snacks, and most importantly, mosquito repellant—there were "zillions" of the tiny bloodsuckers—so many that we had to raise our voices to hear each other over the loud humming noise.

We opted to look for the canoe. Two days later we had recovered it and most of the gear and were on our way again, no worse for wear other than several silver-dollar-sized blisters on Tony's feet and a lost hat and spare paddle. We were fortunate to recover so much of our canoe's contents as we hadn't tied things in and gear scattered over a couple miles in fast muddy water can be quite challenging to find. Lessons three, four, and five: always scout ahead if you aren't certain of conditions, always tie gear securely, and always carry critical emergency items on your person; in a rapidly evolving true emergency, it may be all you are left when you need things the most.

Lessons six and seven were learned in the mid-1980s on a rafting trip but could have just as easily been from a canoeing adventure. On a Friday evening at the start of Memorial Day weekend, Shannon dropped Glenn Elison, his three-year-old son Travis, and me off at the Chatanika River crossing on the Steese Highway north of Fairbanks. Glenn was the Refuge Manager of Arctic National Wildlife Refuge at the time and our families enjoyed a lot of adventures together. We planned a three-day float trip downriver to an access point at the end of Murphy Dome Road. Glenn and I left his pickup near the takeout site a few days earlier but had parked it just shy of the landing to avoid crossing a nasty mud hole and risk getting stuck.

The first day was ideal—a leisurely float in the comforts of a well-stocked Avon Redshank raft. The weather was warm, birds were singing the songs of spring, a campfire was easily started and enjoyed as the woods were dry but not so dry as to risk the fire's escape, and mosquitos had not yet emerged. By mid-day on day two, the river changed. It flattened out and we had to row to make decent time. Soon we encountered thin sheet ice on some of the river bends. The first ones we easily pushed away with the oars but by evening we were portaging raft and gear across small peninsulas (around frozen river corners) to reach flowing water. Just a little of that activity quickly became wearing, but it didn't matter much as our last efforts left us just upstream of a completely frozen river ahead. We set up camp and waited.

After we were a day overdo we heard an airplane approaching and we hopped in the raft and moved out midstream to the edge of the ice and held the boat there. What a sight that must have been to the pilot. Rod King, a pilot-biologist for the Migratory Bird Program, circled a few times and dipped the wings and flew away. Later that evening we heard the hum of a jet boat for nearly an hour before it appeared. Rod Simmons, from the Fairbanks Fisheries Office, roared around the last corner and eased up to the beach where we had the deflated raft and the rest of the gear packed and ready. A little embarrassed, and a whole lot hungry, we loaded the boat and began the long ride back upriver to the Steese Highway. Lessons six and seven were learned: always, always take extra food when striking off on an Alaska adventure, even if only planned for a few days, and always make sure you can reasonably get to where you wish to finish your trip before you actually start it (duh)!

Shannon, like me, had not grown up with any canoeing experience, but she was a fellow wildlife graduate from Oregon State and was adventurous in her own right. One of her early jobs was to work as a foreign fisheries observer for months out in the Gulf of Alaska on a Russian trawler! She took to the Alaska lifestyle quickly and spent her time going back to school at the University of Alaska, working for local small businesses, and taking care of our Airedale and assorted sled dogs. She liked the idea of getting out and seeing the country via canoe and so we planned a Fourth of July trip with the Elisons and began to practice in preparation. We started on the flat water of the Chena River and progressed to the Chatanika River, first with areas with a little current and finally to locations that had both current and obstacles. Feeling pretty good about it all we struck off on our planned trip to cross the Tangle Lakes and down the headwaters of the Delta River.

We paddled across the lakes and camped the first evening and remember Glenn and Denise's two children (Heather and Travis) celebrating the holiday with sparklers and hot dogs around a campfire. The next morning included a short portage of gear around an extended small waterfall to where we would run a series of rapids and be on our way. Shannon and I scouted the river and discussed our route and strategy to avoid boulders, whirlpools, and high waves. I assured her it looked worse than it was. We launched the canoe and were off, paddling hard and weaving in and around hazards. It was all going so well until I shouted to "not worry about the canoe wrapped around the rock ahead, just paddle hard right." Wrong thing to say. There was a silver Grumman canoe, identical to the one we sat in, except it was wrapped around a rock like a horseshoe at the bottom of the river—it couldn't be ignored. Shannon stopped paddling and stared downward and we hit the

rock and wedged solid. We sat there for a time and nothing budged no matter how hard we paddled or pushed off with our paddles. Soon, Glenn and
family came by in their raft and shouted to see if they could help. Of course
there was nothing they could do as they were quickly carried downstream
into the canyon and bobbed safely out of sight. What a predicament. We
were stuck in the middle of the river in serious rapids and couldn't budge an
inch. After giving it some thought I told Shannon we needed to redistribute
our weight, carefully, and change the pivot point. We would accomplish this
by crawling toward each other, switching positions, and proceed backward
if loosened, and then paddle hard to avoid the next hazard immediately
downstream. After a few questioning glances, she agreed and we undertook
the exercise, freeing the canoe and proceeding downstream. Within an hour
we were out of any challenging water and were rewarded by great wildlife
viewing (I remember eagles and caribou particularly) and fantastic grayling
fishing. Shannon, however, never went canoeing with me again.

***

The Yukon River is not known for having dangerous water except for a few
smaller rapids in the upper reaches and an occasional whirlpool that can
take your craft round and round until it decides to spit you out. The biggest
hazard the river holds is its sheer size. With a half mile or more wide in places,
wind can treat the river like a lake and create serious waves and whitecaps (or
in case of the Yukon "browncaps"). The current too, though often running
fairly close to a bank, can switch to mid-stream, thereby taking you a great
distance from shore and from safety should a mishap occur. The outrigger
system I fashioned for my canoe was probably unnecessary I thought, but
in fact it was needed on multiple occasions and worked well. I had cut and
drilled a two by six and lashed it in the mid-section, and then securely tied
a metal pole to the wood. Two Styrofoam fishing floats were secured to the
extended section and an inflatable float was fixed to the short side. If the
boat tipped either way it would be prevented from turning over.

Wind became a problem mid-way through the trip. Wildfires were everywhere and sometimes the wind helped move the smoke away from the river but just as often the opposite occurred. A couple of nights I slept on islands watching black spruce flare up like Roman candles across the channel and would choke on dense air throughout the night. Generally one can expect the wind to pick up in the afternoon and die down at night. When I started getting behind schedule, fighting the wind, I opted to try and nap during the day and paddle at night. But the wind didn't die down then either, it just blew all the time. Generally I would fight it for a while if I was making any progress, but sometimes I would just give up and wait. The wind got me into a predicament three times. The first time was when a crosswind blew me into a slough which upon scouting I learned did not reconnect to the main river. In order to get back out into the main stem I had to paddle into the wind out far enough from the bank to avoid a series of sweepers and fast, rough water. I simply had to wait that one out—nearly six hours before the wind subsided enough to clear the obstacles safely. The second incident occurred when another crosswind kept blowing me ashore along a steep-sloped beach. I couldn't paddle hard enough to prevent the wind from pushing me ashore. Normally in those kind of cases I simply hopped out of the canoe and walk along side for a bit, pulling the canoe along on a rope. One doesn't make much time using this technique but it is nice to stretch your legs and break up a long day of sitting. In this case, however, the bank was too steep and the substrate too muddy. I couldn't get out of the canoe without sinking over my head so I just held it against the bank, again until the wind shifted enough so that I could escape. That time I was "trapped" for only a couple of hours.

The most harrowing event during the trip was when the wind was pushing me hard to shore and the shore was on fire. Most of the time the wildfires were on the hillside, far in the distance, or if they had burned to the river's edge they were then just charred trees, or only still smoldering slightly. In this case however, the whole north bank was aflame and trees were seemingly exploding and toppling into the river in great number. This was fine to watch at a distance but in this case the wind was pushing me hard into the inferno. To further complicate things, rapids were evident from about 50 to 200 feet away from the bank for as far ahead as I could see. If I stayed off shore I would be in the middle of the wind-driven rapids; if I got too close to shore, I was in danger of burning trees toppling onto me. The usual laissez-faire attitude I had moving down river changed quickly. The wind was pushing me into the rapids/fire danger zone and from where I sat I had limited choices. Fighting the wind to go to the south or back upstream was not an option.

I was hugging the shore as much as I dared when a burning tree came down and splashed the canoe. I steered more into the current and tried to hold it there and the waves increased. I paddled through it for a short distance but the wave height continued to increase. No longer could the canoe recover from the last roller before the next struck. The canoe started to fill with water and became sluggish to paddle. I eased it back toward shore and beached among smoldering trees. I then bailed as fast as I could, untied the gear, tipped out the remaining water, reloaded, and struck off quickly to fight through the fast water and to safety. I was successful, but fought the wind and waves for nearly two more hours. During the entire episode I breathed a sigh of relief every time I saw the outrigger float dip into the water and stabilize the canoe. Lesson eight was reinforced: know your equipment and its limitations and do not exceed them.

Shannon loved Alaskan adventures, but decided sled dogs were more fun than canoeing.

Glenn and Travis Elison waiting for the Chatanika River ice to melt.

An outrigger can be a wise investment.

Chapter Five:

PROBLEMS AND POLICIES

A lot had changed in the past 40 years, but The Country wasn't one of them, an observation that perhaps ANILCA had accomplished at least some of what it was set out to do. The wildlife was still evident along the riverbanks; I saw fox, bears, moose, wolves, lynx, porcupine, and beaver. The fish wheels and gill nets were still set in the river to catch migrating salmon, and The Country was largely quiet when more than a few miles away from any of the scattered villages.

With the passage of time, however, partly due to increased technology and partly from evolving government bureaucracy, one thing that changed significantly was the life of a federal biologist. When I started in the office in Anchorage in 1978, we had a typing pool to prepare correspondence, there were no fax machines, "Xerox" copying was handled by a third party, and the thought then that someday we would all have desktop computers was pure fantasy. Fieldwork meant just that: often spending months at a time in the field. Risks were very real in field operations, but they seemed largely to be mitigated by common sense and experience. Tragic accidents, or the threat of them, eventually lead to the creation of one policy and then another. When I started with FWS I had four hours of defensive driving training (one time) before getting a government driver's license. That was it. When I left Alaska 30 years later, I had over 40 hours of required training annually.

The only newly created policy I recall that did not require some training was for communications. The policy simply required each field crew to attempt to make contact daily with a reliable person in town (somewhere). This was a common sense edict and was in response to an incident in the Arctic National Wildlife Range in 1979 (to become the Arctic National Wildlife Refuge with the passage of ANILCA). An archeologist, doing contract work, suffered a massive heart attack and died near the field camp set up along the Beaufort Sea coast. There was nothing that could have been done to save him, but not having any reliable means of communicating from the camp meant the rest of the crew had to spend many days with the victim before his body could be transported. That must have been awful. Of course having a policy that required a daily communication attempt did not assure daily communications actually occurred. One set-up worked well: a heavy Motorola radio; a 12-volt car battery; an extendable fiberglass "hot stick" antenna; gas, generator, and charger for the battery; and rope and wires to secure the antenna. Of course such a package could not be used on raft or canoe trips and had limited value for camps that moved regularly via bush plane or helicopter. The alternative was a Spilsbury radio, about the size of two Kleenex boxes combined, and powered by D-cell batteries. The antenna for the Spilsbury was a finely braided wire rolled onto a small spool. It was deployed by stringing it up on anything you could reach for as far as you could stretch it. Even with the antenna set up in the best way possible, the unit rarely made contact with civilization from most field locations, but we did make our daily attempt to follow policy. The one exception I remember (in actually making contact with someone while using the smaller radio from the North Slope of Alaska) was occasionally we would experience a "skip" and would talk to folks at an FWS camp on Tern Island. The island is in the French Frigate Shoals, hundreds of miles northwest of Honolulu. While we laughed about it at the time, any contact was good, and an emergency message would have certainly been relayed.

Probably the most "out-of-touch" I ever experienced for an extended period was on a trip to Wrangel Island—about an hour's ride via helicopter north of the Siberian coast in the Soviet Union. This was in 1990 but Russian technology available at the time was largely WWII era technology and off-limits to fellow American biologist David Ward and me anyway. After completing a month on the island banding snow geese and black brant (and fitting some of the brant with radio transmitters) we returned to the closest mainland community and learned from our Russian hosts that an unpredictable event had occurred while we were in the field. Our ride back to Provideniya, where our Bering Air charter was to pick us up and fly us to Nome, was no longer available. Apparently sometime in recent weeks a foreign national had been killed in a crash of an Antonov An-2 biplane and Moscow had decreed that they were not to be used by foreigners until further notice. Our flight was to be on such an aircraft and we did not have the funds to charter a helicopter. Several days transpired before we developed a new plan but we had to communicate with Bering Air back in Alaska to revise our charter pickup time. Phone calls were possible but they had to be scheduled a day in advance and could only be undertaken from the telephone building in town where an operator dialed the number for you and physically connected your line via patch cord. Eventually a deal was cut and communicated and we were on our way. We split the cost of chartering a helicopter with a KGB colonel who we dropped en route at a remote outpost (similar to the U.S. Cold War Distant Early Warning "DEW Line" camps). Apparently the KGB figured saving a few dollars was worth the risk of taking a couple Americans (briefly) to one of their facilities. When we got to Nome I called my wife on a real phone and was back to Anchorage and then Cold Bay two days later.

Technology continued to change. By the late 1980s satellite communications were possible, though a typical unit then was only used for bigger operations, such as for a large camp set up to manage a wildfire in a remote location. The satellite phone system was unwieldly, had its own dish, and had to be slung with a helicopter on a pallet to the camp. Come 2019, things were much more advanced and simpler. While cell phones work in much of the world, most of rural Alaska is still without coverage. Satellite technology, however, has advanced to the point that one can communicate anywhere at any time with a device that will fit in a shirt pocket. I was carrying two such devices while paddling the Upper Yukon, one in a waterproof pouch in a fanny pack that I took off only when I crawled into the sleeping bag at night, the second in a waterproof bag and float tethered to a loop on my life jacket. The Garmin InReach Explorer allowed me to text with my wife, check my location with GPS map overlay, request immediate rescue if ever needed, and a whole lot more. Times had changed indeed!

FWS policies addressing aviation and boating safety had origins similar to the communications policy—people had died. Each story is significant and hopefully lessons were learned and similar accidents avoided in the future. At the FWS National Conservation Training Center (Shepherdstown, West Virginia), a memorial wall stands with Service employee names who died while in the line of work. A disproportionate amount of them are Alaska Region employees, and most of them met their end either flying or boating. I knew many of them, and their memories return particularly fresh whenever I travel in bush Alaska. In the case of the Yukon Flats National Wildlife Refuge, the assistant manager two before me, Rich Barcelona, drowned when his canoe overturned while conducting duck brood counts, and the assistant manager second after me, Steve Young, was killed while flying a winter moose survey. There were others—far too many. While I remember the days well when mandatory safety training was all but non-existent, I never complained about boating and aviation training efforts. If they saved one employee's life in the future, and prevented all the grief and stress that follows such a loss, they were well worth it.

BEARS

There was one policy developed that did not have its origin with an employee death. The original policy for safety when working in bear country was written after a regional office employee was reviewing year-end purchase requests from the field and was struck by the number and diversity of requests for different firearms that employees desired to protect them and others from bears. The reviewer felt that standardized weaponry and training should be a matter of policy and so another well-meaning policy was born. I must add here that outside of some fundamental political disagreements, perhaps nothing creates a louder debate in rural Alaska than views about what constitutes the best bear gun. In fact, the U.S. Forest Service even published a peer-reviewed scientific article on the topic, concluding (if I remember correctly) that the .458 Winchester Magnum was the best bear stopper device, but since the recoil could not be managed effectively by many who might find themselves in a precarious situation in the bush, the .375 H&H Magnum was the recommended choice. There was also some discussion of the 12-gauge shotgun with slugs as being acceptable, but in second place to a rifle.

One might think that over time some field biologist met their demise by a bear in Alaska, and although many individuals have been killed by bears, and I have had employees who have been attacked (both on and off duty), I am unaware of any biologist being killed by a bear in Alaska. That's not to say that there are no significant risks to address or a comprehensive policy was not warranted. It did suggest, however, that the policy need weigh the risks of being chewed on by a bear with the risks of arming everyone who worked in bear country (essentially all of Alaska). Quite a number of the younger seasonal employees I helped train for fieldwork had little or no previous experience with firearms.

Firearm safety was the first order of business, followed by proficiency. The policy evolved and grew to the point that basic training was required and annual proficiency to be demonstrated. If one was to work alone in the field. If you were working with others, at least one person, working closely with you, must have demonstrated proficiency for that year and was properly equipped, consistent with policy. For ease of training, dependability in various climatic conditions and under stress, and for manageable recoil, the 12-gauge pump shotgun was the weapon of choice (loaded with slugs).

To pass the proficiency test the shooter had to put two out of three rounds into the vitals of a charging bear target in a few seconds (the target being the frontal outline of a grizzly bear being hurled toward you with a cable and pulley system). In truth, the exercise was not bad, but it in no way mimicked a true bear charge. For one, it was paper, not flesh and bone; second, as fast as it was, it was much much slower than a real charging bear; third, the shooter was ready, whereas in real charges, there is rarely much if any warning; and finally, while there is some stress trying to perform acceptably in front of your peers on the shooting range, the intensity of a true bear attack can create unimaginable fear. Still, the training was probably as good as it could have been and I know of at least three attacks that ended up in dead bears and uninjured field biologists.

Part of the later bear policy included the requirement to carry deterrents as well as the lethal means of dealing with a bear. Hand-held flares were popular for a while but were soon discovered to be an unacceptable fire risk in dry conditions. I myself had the embarrassment of shutting down the Alaska Department of Fish and Game (ADF&G) Rabbit Creek shooting range when a fire erupted over the berm from a flare I was demonstrating at a bear safety training session. Air horns can work too and I like to carry one to try and dissuade a curious bear or to use to alert others to my location in a potential emergency. I say "can" work, in that I have seen bears "beat feet" at the blast of an air horn and have seen others totally ignore the noise. In one case, when a young grizzly bear was taking too much of a liking to our camp, we tried air horns and flares. The bear would sit down like a circus bear and watch and listen with no real concern. Finally, several of us (also being well armed) charged the bear and it turned and took off and never looked back. In some ways bears are like people. They have different personalities and have good days and bad days. I know some studies can help understand bear behavior and how to deter potential attacks, but I know too that true attacks on humans are an anomaly and so are difficult to predict by studying "normal" bear behavior.

While manager of Izembek National Wildlife Refuge in Cold Bay, the staff and I sometimes dealt with problem bears as we were the only full-time wildlife officials for over a hundred miles. The brown bears there grew large, although the same species, I generally referred to brown bears of interior and northern Alaska as "grizzlies" and the larger coastal brown bears of southeast Alaska, Kodiak, and the Alaska Peninsula as just brown bears. If a brown bear became too habituated to town, or would hang out too long close to a home, people would often call and ask us to deal with "our bear." We never killed any of the animals and tried to use cracker shells and rubber bullets, usually together, as a deterrent. I would load the shotgun chamber with a rubber bullet, followed by a cracker shell in the magazine, and then three live rounds (sabot slugs). The goal was to approach close enough to the bear while yelling at it and hope it ran off. You definitely didn't want to surprise the bear, but rather let it see you coming. If it didn't run away, when close enough to effectively use the rubber bullet, I would shoot the bear in the butt and immediately pump in the next round and fire the pyrotechnic round over the (hopefully fleeing) bear, and then just as quickly pump in a live round and prepare for the worst (which thankfully never happened). What did happen one time though, after I smacked a bear in the butt and fired the cracker shell over its head, the spent pyrotechnic shell didn't eject and I was unable to load the slug. The cracker shells were inexpensive Chinese import pyrotechnics (producing a flash and a bang) and had plastic rather than brass hulls, and the gun's ejector had stripped through the plastic, leaving the empty round stuck in the barrel. My heart skipped a beat as I realized that I was helpless if the bear turned back, but it didn't. After that though I changed tactics. The preferred determent operation then required two trained people—one operating the shotgun and the other standing by as backup with an iron-sighted .375 H&H magnum rifle. Fortunately we were never required to use the rifle.

Pyrotechnic-type rounds can work well but they too are not perfect. I once witnessed a sow polar bear succumb to the wounds from such a round that wasn't even fired directly toward her, but it spun wildly and exploded against her belly killing her sometime during the night and orphaning her two cubs.

The most common bear determent these days, besides perhaps traditional bear bells hanging from one's pack, is pepper spray. It has been used enough over the years now that data suggest, for the average person and bear encounter, it can be more effective than a firearm in dissuading a charging bear. This makes some sense as a can of bear spray is more easily kept readily available than most guns; it sprays a wide fog of seriously irritating particles rather than a single small projectile to hit the target, and it often comes with a dye so you can see where the spray is being deployed. That said, I still take both a firearm and bear spray when in serious bear country. Bear spray is ineffective if windy conditions are not favorable to the direction you need to spray, and once the can's contents are exhausted it can't be reloaded.

The very best defense against bear attacks is avoiding close encounters in the first place. This is most easily done by making noise when moving through thick brush and by keeping a clean camp—cooking and storing food away from your tent. Bears are curious and have an incredible sense of smell, something we cannot even begin to imagine. I was reminded of this from time to time; once during the Exxon Valdez oil spill when sampling tissue from a gray whale washed up on Sanak Island and finding two brown bears already there—they would have had to swim across approximately 30 miles of open ocean to reach the carcass (an incredible food source for them) and the only way they could have known it was there was by smelling it from the shores of Unimak Island (the first in the Aleutian Chain). Similar situations occur almost annually in places like Kaktovik where a polar bear won't be seen for months within many miles near the village, but within a day or two of a bowhead whale being harvested and drug ashore, multiple bears just seem to pop up. Knowing that even residual food smells could trigger a bear to investigate a camp, another deterrent available these days can also make good sense—that is a small portable D-cell powered electric fence. I highly recommend such devices for longer term camps, but they can't replace common sense.

When managing a national wildlife refuge in Alaska one can expect to have a lot of discussions with visitors about bears. One such extended conversation I remember lasted on and off via telephone for months before a New Mexico couple arrived In Cold Bay. They were looking for what they hoped would be the rawest wilderness left in the United States, had done a great deal of research, and had chosen Unimak Island to visit. Early phone conversations with the adventurers focused on remoteness, routes, and scenery, but always seemed to come back to questions about bears. Unimak was certainly wild: only the small fishing village of False Pass held any people; it was scenic too, with striking mountains, river valleys, and a continuously smoking volcano. And while there were caribou and wolves to be seen on occasion, the most prevalent large mammal populating Unimak Island was the brown bear. I advised carrying a firearm as well as assorted deterrent devices, but most importantly, to avoid the dense vegetation along the salmon streams. They opted against a gun, voicing a fairly common wilderness visitor sentiment that, "We are visiting their home" and did not generally believe in the killing of wildlife.

I respected their view but also relayed the story of a man a few years previous that had been camping alone not far from the town of Cold Bay and had been killed and partially eaten during the night. This was not meant to scare them so much as share the facts. Still, they chose to venture off unarmed and with an apparent belief that if they didn't intend to hurt a bear, it should feel the same way about them. Two days after they had departed I had an air taxi pilot swing by the office and drop off a severely shredded backpack. He said something like, "This is all that's left of your backpackers," and then turned and left. To say I was curious at that point is a gigantic understatement. I quickly learned, however, that the couple were safe in False Pass and were aborting their month-long planned wilderness adventure. Apparently they went exactly where I had cautioned not to—to the nearest salmon stream— and set up camp. They did leave all their food and other gear, including their hiking boots, at some distance away but where they could see it from their tent. They got a good show too—a young brown bear came along and helped himself to whatever was of interest and the backpackers crept away undertaking what had to be a pretty uncomfortable walk back to the village without hiking boots.

People are sometimes injured by bears and unfortunately sometimes the injuries result in death. All three species found in Alaska (brown, black, and polar) can cause demise but the brown/grizzly bear is the most feared. In truth, I suspect the polar bear is the most dangerous but humans rarely encounter them in close quarters. That could be changing as oil and gas activities increase, and polar sea ice decreases in the Arctic. Polar bears by nature are predators and capture, kill, and eat meat. Unlike their black and brown cousins, they have little opportunity to supplement their diet with emerging plants, roots, and berries. They also may spend their entire life wandering the ice and rarely encountering people, so when they do come upon one it wouldn't be a surprise for them to consider a person to be a slower version of an upright bearded seal.

Black bears rarely attack people but a surprisingly large number of human fatalities have occurred over time because of them. Invariably older male bears are involved, and their victims are commonly women or youth. Like polar bear attacks, a black bear attack is almost always a predatory action. So while the advice of experts generally is to "play dead" if attacked by a brown/grizzly bear, the same experts suggesting fighting back if attacked by a black bear. I think that is pretty good advice if the critter is intent on making a meal out of you. I can't emphasize enough, however, that black bear attacks are extremely rare and you probably have a greater chance of being struck by lightning than being killed by a black bear.

Brown/grizzly bears have a reputation for being fierce, but most attacks are directly related to defending their young, a food source, or their personal space. While managing the Kenai National Wildlife Refuge over 14 years I would guess we had about five bear "attacks" per year on the refuge and I only remember one being from a black bear (that were much more numerous). To put this in perspective though, over a million people visited the refuge each year and most of the reported encounters did not result in long-term physical injury—some as simple as being knocked down—though I imagine the mental trauma in most cases was long-lasting. One of the non-fatal encounters involved a sow grizzly with cubs near the mouth of the Russian River was quite serious however. A young man was permanently blinded in that attack. Most of the attacks similarly involved sows and cubs, along with close "surprise" encounters. One such incident occurred behind the refuge office one August morning when an employee was jogging on a hiking trail and came around a well-vegetated corner quickly and surprised the bears. Playing dead may sound difficult in such a situation but most often the sow will leave her victim as soon as she feels the person is no longer a threat to her young (and lying flat on the ground motionless is the best way to do this). Even a few seconds, however, of a mauling by a 500-pound creature armed with two-inch teeth and four-inch claws can do serious injury, and people finding themselves in this situation should lie face down in fetal position and clasp their hands tightly behind their neck and then try to remain quiet and still.

Two attacks by brown bears while I was managing the Kenai did result in human fatalities. In both cases adult men were killed (near instantly) by adult male brown bears. The first happened when a winter seismic crew worker stepped in front of a bear den on February 8, 1998, in the Finger Lakes area near Swanson River. The second occurred while a man was heating water with a backpacking stove on the Funny River Horse Trail on May 28, 1999. Both men apparently found themselves in close quarters with bears who bit them once in the head and then departed. A large male brown bear is large enough to get a grip over a person's head and bite down. Females frequently try the same technique but aren't large enough to accomplish it. I remember vividly one report of a young man who had been attacked by a sow brown bear with cubs near Tustumena Lake in May 2003. He said he was tossed about like a rag doll but the worst part was hearing the crunching noise while she bit his head. Ultimately he required an ear to be repaired, multiple stiches in his face, and 38 staples to reattach his scalp, along with wounds needing repair on his arms and thigh and orthopedic surgery on a badly broken hand, but he lived to tell the story.

In traveling thousands of miles in rural Alaska over the years I had my share of bear encounters. Most were positive ones. Two, however, caused an adrenaline rush that I don't care to repeat.

The first occurred along the Kongakut River in the Arctic National Wildlife Refuge. I was part of a four-person fisheries crew doing fisheries and stream survey work and we had been flown in by helicopter to the headwaters in the Brooks Range for what was planned as a two-month stint—floating the entire length of the river, collecting data along the way, and then motoring along the coast to Beaufort Lagoon and continuing work there. The first week of the trip had been uncomfortable. It rained every day and everything we possessed was damp. It had been windy too, but at least this kept the mosquitos down. We were camped near the mouth of the Pagilak River when the weather changed. At about 4 am the sun was shining bright and my tent mate (David Wiswar) and I decided to get up and to hike to the tributary stream and sample it without waking the rest of the crew. It was indeed a beautiful day. The Porcupine Caribou herd was migrating through the valley and their impressive numbers dotted the hillsides. After completing our work we began the half mile or so hike back to our rafts and camp when I felt the urge to undertake my morning constitutional. I waived David ahead and found a small clump of willows to screen me a little from his view and set about to dig a "cat hole" and complete my business.

At some point I swear I had a premonition of an approaching bear, but whether true or not, a real bear did appear over a nearby hill, swaying slightly as he neared my position. He was big, at least for this part of the world, a large silvertip hump evident, along with a dished face, pig-like eyes, and long, very long, yellowish claws. He was not only big, he was close and getting closer. Until that morning I had been carrying a magnum revolver in a shoulder holster, but had left it in the tent thinking that we would be working in open tundra that morning and that we would have our shotgun. David was now carrying the .12 gauge back to camp. My only armament was an aluminum Marsh Mcbirney wading rod used to help collect stream flow measurements. I was now brandishing the rod from a squatting position at the approaching bear. I was yelling too—at the bear, but hoping David would hear. The bear certainly could hear me, but my shouting only seemed to make him more interested as he began to circle me in a somewhat crouched position mere feet away. David was probably no more than 150 meters or so from me but he didn't hear the commotion at first. The tundra was literally alive with breeding bird sounds—primarily dunlin, snow buntings, and Lapland longspurs—also enjoying the bright, sunny day. Eventually though, David did hear and turned back to see me jabbing my makeshift spear in the air towards the approaching grizzly, and shouting what I always did when a bear was approaching: "Hey bear!"

David himself started screaming and running back toward me while he was jacking shells out of the shotgun until it double fed and jammed. In the heat of the moment he had not only not fired the gun but had rendered it useless for a time. No matter, he bravely kept running toward us giving his best Rambo imitation, and the bear, having never witnessed anything even remotely close to this, I am sure, hightailed it back over the hill from which he had come. It took nearly 20 minutes for me to dig apart the stuck shotgun shell using a Swiss army knife to make the weapon useful again, but I did not chastise David—far from it. His actions probably saved me from a pretty unsavory end. Like the rare black bear incidents I previously mentioned, that particular grizzly was exhibiting unlikely predatory behavior, and I was the prey. As a note to gun buffs, Remington soon altered the floorplate on their popular Model 870 shotguns and replaced the solid piece of spring steel with one that is vented in a blunted U-shape. This allows a user who might double feed the weapon in the heat of battle to depress the action release button while slamming the butt stock into the ground. This should bend the floorplate allowing the jammed shell to be cleared quickly and feed a live round into the chamber.

In nearly 30 years of working in bear country I had never had to kill a bear until an incident that occurred on July 31, 2008. I had arrived at the Kenai Refuge office early when a call came in from Larry Lewis with ADF&G. An angler had been charged by a brown bear with cubs near the Sterling Highway in the vicinity of the Russian River Ferry and he had shot at the bear with his .44 magnum and thought he had hit it. Larry was going to meet the fisherman and track the bear and was asking for backup. Normally the refuge had several refuge officers on call but none were currently available. After a short conversation with my assistant Doug Staller, it was decided I would go and help Larry. I grabbed a shotgun and ammo, hip boots, a bottle of water, radio, and bug spray and took off. Larry and I arrived at the same time at the parking area that accessed the "powerline hole" and the angler was waiting there in his vehicle, still visibly shaken. After a short interview we went with him to where the incident had taken place, recovered his fishing gear, walked him back to the parking lot, and then returned to where he had shot the bear. Fairly quickly we found blood, both dark blood and bright red bubbly blood. The bear had been hit at least twice from a few feet away. By then, Duston Beyer, a refuge officer, had arrived to the parking area and I had him close off the area to the public. The second run of sockeye salmon was beginning to peak and the area attracted thousands of anglers. With a wounded bear likely nearby, and one that had already demonstrated aggressive behavior, I didn't want to take any chances with someone else stumbling into the bear in the thick vegetation between the river and the highway while Larry and I were trying to sort things out.

The blood was easy to follow for nearly 75 meters and then it petered out. We did the best we could to follow flattened and broken vegetation while on high alert, once significantly startled as a bull moose jumped from its grassy bed only a short distance away. Suddenly we could hear the bear ahead of us huffing and popping her teeth. She was somewhere behind a downed cottonwood tree and after a bit of commotion she made several bluff charges. On about the third go at it she came full blown over the tree on a dead run and I heard Larry, shout, "Here she comes" as I fired, hitting her front on, almost certainly in the center of a lung. As she spun Larry fired too and the bear fell back over the tree and all went silent. We waited nearly 20 minutes and then heard some skittering. Larry's comment then, "That's not good," was an acknowledgement that a cub or cubs was coming down from a tree and following its wounded mother.

It didn't seem like the situation could get much worse. As we approached the downed tree I don't think I had ever seen so much blood, and I had butchered moose in the snow before. How could anything survive that kind of blood loss and still be alive and moving I thought? But somehow she did. We followed carefully and she just kept going, first parallel to the Highway, and then crossing it. At that point I got Dusty on the radio and asked him to join us. The bear was no longer a threat to the public by the river and we could use him, his training, and his .30 caliber semi-automatic rifle.

The three of us tracked the bear easily for another two hours. Since it was moving away from the public use area I felt that the risk to the public was continuing to diminish. Our goal now would be to put the bear out of her misery if possible. This needed to be balanced with our own safety. We had been at it a long while, our reaction time was likely starting to slow, we were following uphill through brush, and the bear knew we were in pursuit. We agreed to give it one more hour. Most of that time had passed when without any warning the loudest roar you could imagine erupted from thick grass a few feet ahead of us as the bear leapt forward at lightning fast speed. We all fired, a lot, and the bear fell dead at our feet.

Emotions running high, we skinned the bear and did a cursory necropsy. At least one of the 300 grain .44 Magnum bullets had penetrated her gastrointestinal area – she would have likely died slowly from that wound. Another handgun slug had passed through the bear's nose and penetrated the sternum on the chest, but lodged under the pericardial lining without penetrating the heart. If the bullet had been a solid rather than a hollow point, the whole incident would have likely ended near the riverbank eight hours earlier. Such things happen and we were glad no one was physically injured in the ordeal. The saddest part of the story was the fate of the cubs—the sow had three small male cubs of the year. They had to be euthanized. They were too young to survive on their own and rehabilitation centers and zoos weren't taking any more—ADF&G kept good track of such facilities as needs always arose each year to house bear cubs as well as moose calves, usually orphaned from vehicle collisions. The story ends then unhappily with five victims: the fishermen who was traumatized but protected his own life, the mother brown bear that acted in defense of her young, and ultimately, the young bears too.

In the long run, bears in Alaska are part of the reason it is an interesting place. I had hundreds of encounters with bears over the years, and enjoyed most of them. When visitors expressed worries about bears I would remind them that the odds of having a problem were extremely remote—be smart and have fun. For a few folks though, the fears they held could not be reasonably overcome and they did not enjoy their visit. That is too bad. When conversations from worried visitors became extended and seemed to be a lost cause, I might teasingly say something like, "If you want to be remembered, be eaten by a bear; if you want to be forgotten, die at home in front of the television. " I know, however, such jesting was not helpful.

Banding black brant – Wrangel Island, USSR.

Bear encounters often happen without warning.

Chapter Six:

FIRE AND ICE

Wildfires in Interior Alaska are not a new phenomenon. When I was the Assistant Refuge Manager at Yukon Flats National Wildlife Refuge in 1988, over a million acres of the Refuge's boreal forest burned that year. That was the year Yellowstone National Park burned too (with all fires there consuming about 800,000 acres). A lot of people remember the Yellowstone fires but I imagine there are very few that remember the fires on the Flats that year—something pretty indicative of a lot of events in Alaska, but most Alaskans preferred it that way. The fires were natural, ignited by lightning and fueled by dry windy conditions. Black spruce seems to burn naturally every 70 years or so, plus or minus a couple decades. I expected to see smoke on my 2019 trip too, and ample evidence of old and recent burns. What I did not expect was to witness active fires through most of my several-hundred-mile journey and have the fires dictate where I would camp and even where I would try to paddle on more days than not.

Alaska was experiencing a particularly warm and dry summer. Drought conditions were evident from the Kenai Peninsula to the Yukon Flats. Cottonwood and alder leaves were brown and stiff rather than green and glistening. And it was hot. Anchorage saw July temperatures exceed 90 degrees Fahrenheit for the first time ever. While visiting my daughter Alex on the Fourth of July weekend, her interior thermometer registered 104 degrees and Alaskans don't have air conditioning in their homes. Call it pessimism or just being realistic, the Arctic is warming about twice as fast as the rest of the planet and its effects cannot be ignored. And while fire in interior Alaska is not at all new, and is a critical natural process, the length and intensity of the fire season is new and dramatic.

Other than the times the wind pushed my canoe into active fire zones along the riverbank, canoeing down the Yukon River was generally safe even as it passed through numerous large wildfires. The River overall provided a pretty darn good fire break, and offered long, sandy beaches, away from flammable vegetation, as well as countless islands dotted throughout the many wandering channels. Finding a safe place to camp wasn't a problem, though it didn't always come when I was otherwise ready to stop for the day. Avoiding getting burned was therefore fairly easy—getting away from the smoke was another thing. The acrid smell of wood smoke never really disappeared. Even when the wind would push the smoke away from the river for a time, its residue clung to the lining of my nostrils and reminded me that it wasn't really going anywhere anytime soon. In the worst cases, the smoke was not only thick but the sky was full of floating ash as heavier cinders popped and fizzled as they fell into the muddy water surrounding the canoe. At these times I used a bandana around my nose and mouth to filter out the thicker particles, though it probably didn't really help much. On two mornings, after particularly smoky nights, I awoke with my eyelids stuck together from weepy secretions—my eyes stinging and reddened in protest of the smoke. The conditions did provide for some of the most spectacular sunrises and sunsets however—surreal explosions of fiery brightness filtered through a bluish-gray haze.

For the most part, all fires in Alaska are monitored, and managed as necessary, but not actively fought. Managers of Wilderness areas follow policies to allow fire to take its natural role in the ecosystem so they generally suppress human-caused ignitions and let lightning-ignited fires burn as much as practicable. Human life is clearly the number one priority in fire management operations but other factors come into play too, such as the protection of culturally important sites and other resource values. Outside of Wilderness, managers may choose to let certain fires burn to meet particular objectives also. At Kenai I frequently let fires burn away from communities but aggressively fought fires that threatened structures and people. We generally experienced a large "Type I or Type II" fire, requiring incident management teams and a large amount of personnel and equipment, every two or three years. While all the fires were managed, allowing some fires to burn for resource benefit was labelled "let burn" by the media and frequently came under attack. One particular time I remember being interviewed live, with a television camera stuck in my face, about my decision to not suppress a particular fire that was close to Soldotna, but burning away from town. A controlled burn conducted by the BLM near Fairbanks had been in the news recently because it had escaped its planned burn area and subsequently was being actively fought so it didn't come any closer to town. I was being asked if I wasn't afraid the same thing would happen to the Kenai fire. I replied, "No" to which the reporter of course asked, "Why not?" I then said, "Because Fairbanks is over 500 miles away..." Fortunately the reporter shook her head, slid a hand across her throat signaling the cameraman to cut, and walked away, but I knew immediately my flippant comment was inappropriate. There is nothing funny about wildfires and a seasoned reporter would have kept the camera rolling and pursued me all the more on the subject. In fact, I did resent the media sometimes sensationalizing fire events and fueling the flames of public opinion away from pertinent facts, but I should have stuck to topic. Not actively suppressing every fire allows for resource benefit, reduces risks to firefighters, and saves taxpayers a bundle of money. Those reasons should be justification enough for not putting out every fire. Another benefit over time too is, "a fire survived is a fire that protects"—that is, a fire can't burn hot for many years in the future over an area that has had most of its flammable vegetation already consumed. Successfully managed fires around communities create great fire breaks. It is especially nice when Mother Nature pays the bills for these community safeguards too.

———————————

As I paddled downstream far away from any community, I knew that fire managers had large latitude for managing most of the fires in the Country and down into the Flats. The Alaska Fire Service, working under a delegation of authority from the appropriate federal land manager, would monitor and protect around villages, historic cabins, and likely a few other features on the land. Trapping cabins might be protected, if they knew of their existence, but I didn't know the current policy on such things. I did know though that whether the cabins were protected or not, the traplines themselves would likely change significantly. Downed trees after a fire can make travel by snow machine difficult early in winter, and more importantly, furbearer distribution can be drastically altered. With mature spruce trees being lost, red squirrels' population declines and the marten that prey upon them will be hard to come by for years to come. On the other hand, a new burn allows a burst of willow, birch, and aspen to grow which prompt an increase in snowshoe hares, and increases in lynx numbers follow.

Yes, it was a big fire year. I don't know how many acres burned within the Yukon–Charley Rivers Natural Preserve in 2019, but Jimmy Fox (Yukon Flats Refuge Manager) informed me that over 500,000 acres of the Refuge had burned by the time I had completed my trip, and there were over 1,700 lightning strikes the night before I departed. More fire was on the way.

———————————

I thought often of the changes fire brings as I scanned the passing shoreline from my canoe and I frequently spied fallen trees that had been sawn off a few feet above ground. This was a good reminder that, while the forest was on fire then, in a few short months the Yukon will once again freeze solid and become a highway for snow machines and dog teams. The sawn trees are the remnants of firewood collected by snowmobile and sled, often 30 or more miles from a village. The constantly eroding riverbanks produce a replenished wood supply by toppling trees into the Yukon's edge which then become easily accessible as the water levels drop and then freeze. Climate change threatens that too. No longer can one simply look at the calendar and decide when it is safe to travel on what should be frozen lakes and rivers. Freeze-up is coming later and the thaw earlier. The Yukon River is the transportation highway of interior Alaska—watercraft in summer and snow machine and dog team in winter but the shoulder season offers safe travel with none of these and the shoulder season is growing longer. A very unscientific way of examining the prospect of a changing early breakup, is looking at the Nenana Ice Classic—an Alaskan gambling tradition that allows people to bet on when a tripod on the Tanana River will tip. Last year it fell on April 14, by far the earliest since the contest started in 1917. The next earliest ice out date in the 102-year history of the Nenana Ice Classic was April 20; the latest breakup recorded was May 20.

Breakup is a celebrated time in Alaska and watching the ice go out on an Alaskan river can be a spectacular experience. It is also a bit humbling, making one feel small and insignificant. Alaska celebrates its ice in other ways too—many of its glaciers are significant tourist attractions. The pace of receding of Alaska glaciers foretells the loss of not only their huge fresh-water source and special sites to be visited and photographed but also loss to an irreplaceable storehouse of scientific data. Like examining tree rings to determine its age, coring a glacier can reveal annual or periodic deposits of pollen, volcanic ash, insect parts, and soot from wildfires—some of these records going back thousands of years.

My personal memories of snow and ice are many. Some of them were subtle, like melting my frozen moustache and beard with what my tongue could reach when cross-country skiing on a frosty day. Others were more intense, such as being awakened at night by the roar of the icepack shifting while I camped on a barrier island in the Beaufort Sea (a phenomenon now absent as the sea ice is no longer close to shore in the summer); or the large mosaic of shapes formed by slowly freezing saltwater seen when flying low over Cook Inlet on a winter's day; or the mesmerizing pattern of snowflakes hitting your car windshield when driving in a blizzard—something akin to a prolonged view of "jumping to light speed" in a *Star Wars* movie.

Snow is nearly ubiquitous for all of Alaska—the variation is only in how much and for how long. In the eight years we lived in Fairbanks, we only experienced one winter with enough snow that I had to use tire chains. It was always cold there though—one winter dropped to more than 60 degrees below zero for a spell and I remember getting a call from Shannon from town to come and get her after the diaphragm on her clutch shattered when she tried to shift into gear in order to drive home from work. I left the cabin and uncovered my car, confident it would be fine as I had it "plugged in" with a block heater (to warm the oil), a battery warmer (to ensure full battery power), and an electric heater (to keep the cabin from freezing to the point things broke—an earlier event of hopping in a frozen vehicle and pumping the gas pedal before trying to start it resulted in a shattered gas pedal—rubber transforms to a glass-like substance in extreme cold). My car did start fine, but the clutch would not engage and I couldn't move forward or backward. I called Shannon back and said she would need to stay in town until things warmed a bit. Rather fond but childish memories of life at the cabin on cold nights included peeing off the deck and watching the urine crackle and freeze before it hit the snow below (this is one of those things you can try at home if it is cold enough and the neighbors don't mind).

Snowy winters were more common when living in Anchorage or Soldotna. There, about every five or six winters, enough snow fell that one would has to shovel their roof to prevent potential catastrophe. People who owned boats moored at Seward or Whittier, or airplanes not stored in a hanger, either had their vessels cleaned of snow or risked them being sunk or wings torn off in those heavy snow years. One wintry morning in Anchorage I awoke to a clatter on the roof and it wasn't Rudolf. It was however a cow moose. The snow around the house was deep enough she had stepped up on top of the two-story home and was trying to browse the top of a mountain ash tree in our yard.

In Cold Bay, snow was not so much a factor as the wind. It seemingly blew constantly there—even a small amount of snow, under such windy conditions, drifted in ways difficult to imagine. During one storm we stacked truck tires on the roof of our office and one of the government houses to keep the metal from peeling off in winds gusting over 100 mph. I also remember Mike Blenden (the assistant manager at the time) assisting me to close the double entrance doors to my home—the double doors were to help prevent brown bears from breaking in. Shannon was away giving birth to our first child and alone I could not clear the heavy, wet snow away quickly enough, as it blew horizontally and cemented to the door jam, to get it closed and latched. Mike assisted from outside while I rapidly cleaned from within. After that experience we had Arctic entryways built for our homes.

Another time I boarded a Reeve Aleutian Airways plane to fly to Anchorage and when doing so there wasn't a sign of snow on the ground or in the air. Shortly before takeoff, a squall blew through the area and we waited it out onboard, engines still running. A little over an hour later the flight was cancelled and the passengers disembarked. We couldn't move the plane due to the snow that had accumulated in the short time since board-ing—we offloaded out the cargo door onto a box held by a forklift. Another time upon landing in Cold Bay (in a 727), a gust of wind hit us when taxiing and stuck the jet in a snow drift on the east side of the runway. Passengers remained onboard, again for about an hour, while a call was made to Boeing to determine a safe way to winch us free without damaging the aircraft.

My strongest memory of drifting snow in Cold Bay does not involve an airplane but rather a car. After one stormy night of wispy snow and strong winds, I found that I had to spend nearly two hours to dig my vehicle out of a drift. That probably doesn't sound so incredible unless I also mention that the vehicle was in the garage with the door down. Snow had blown through a crack no more than a half-inch high and piled up several feet from the garage floor and around my vehicle like wet concrete.

Over the years much debate has taken place about building a road from Cold Bay to King Cover, through Izembek National Wildlife Refuge, to be used by King Cove residents in case of a medical emergency. It has been my experience that when the weather is good there, one can fly or operate a boat safely; when the weather is poor, you cannot. When the weather is extreme, you can't go anywhere, even by car; within minutes of a grader clearing snow off a local road under such conditions, it would drift over again. The storms, while intense, were usually short-lived, though I do remember one eight-day period in which no flights came in and out and all of the roads around town were drifted in with snow.

Alaskans scrape their windshields, shovel snow, and plug in their cars without complaint in urban areas. In the bush the biggest concern is whether the ice is thick enough to keep you from falling through. I fell through the ice twice over the years. Once while snowshoeing alone along my trapline when I tried to take a shortcut across a frozen slough. Apparently that part of the river was spring-fed and the snow covered backwater was set like a trap itself. The day was very cold, approximately 30 degrees below zero and I was wearing enough layers that the icy water didn't really reach my skin as I floundered and rolled back onto the ice quickly and was able to soak up some of the water in light fluffy snow, which quickly froze to my parka and bibs. Once safe though, my movements were probably quite comical to watch. My clothing was frozen stiff and I walked along like having stovepipe wrapped around both legs.

The other time I fell through the ice was a bit more dramatic, but also without witnesses, though several young Yupik hunters were nearby.

SAVOONGA

In May and June 1980, I found myself on St. Lawrence Island at the village of Savoonga. I was there to help monitor subsistence walrus hunting. Since about 1959 and until then, ADF&G had conducted this type of work, but the Marine Mammal Protection Act had recently been reauthorized and some of the changes did not set well with the State—they drop-kicked a great deal of management back to the feds, not wanting to operate with the newly legislated restrictions. One of the biggest changes was that non-Natives were no longer legally permitted to hunt walrus. I quickly came to appreciate this concern too, not in support of sport hunting opportunity, but in consideration of walrus conservation. Native people acted as guides for visiting hunters and made good money, and the take was strictly regulated by quota. Without that income, more walrus would seemingly be taken as ivory was the major source of income for many. While meat could be had from birds, seals, walrus, and whales, cash was needed to buy other food items, medicine, fuel oil, clothing, ammunition, and other supplies. The people living on St. Lawrence Island were excellent carvers and a good portion of their livelihood depended on a readily available source of ivory.

A government pilot, flying a Cessna 337 (push-pull) aircraft, took me to the island from Nome and dropped me off in the middle of a snowstorm at the end of a gravel airstrip, about a mile from the village. My only contact was an elder named Alexander Akeya and when eventually a snow machine appeared from the village I asked its driver where I could find Alex. The reply was a bit of a shock, "He is on the other side of the island whale hunting—don't know when he will be back." So, on my own, with hundreds of pounds of gear and very little money, I set out to find a place to stay and was fortunate to be taken in by the Toolie family—eldest son Warren would let me stay with him and he would be reimbursed via a contract I had with Kawerak. Kawerak, Inc. was the nonprofit arm of the Bering Straits Native Corporation (created by ANCSA). While there, I was to monitor the walrus harvest and to purchase samples from willing hunters: I paid (indirectly through Kawerak) $6 for a pair of teeth, $15 for female reproductive tracts, and $50 for a stomach. The stomachs could weigh nearly 100 pounds and I would sub-sample the contents and return them to the hunter who then might use them to make a drum. Walrus feed by propelling themselves along the sea floor, probing the substrate with their tusks, and use their bulbous lips to literally suck the necks and feet from mollusks with very little shell being ingested. I remember some of the Yupik children watching me with the stomach sampling, with some of them occasionally sneaking in and grabbing some of the partially digested clams and popping them in their mouths like candy—giggling as green juices ran down their chins. That may sound gross but the mollusk parts probably tasted pretty good – probably not that much different than gulping down a raw oyster.

Food in the village was mostly what came from the land. There was a small village store but it had few items and they were very expensive. This was a factor for me too. I had brought all the provisions I would need for the time I was to be in the village but most of the food was eaten by locals within a few days. The cultural differences were stark. People were quiet and friendly but came and went from each other's homes without ever knocking or announcing themselves and food was to be shared without question. My biggest fear, however, was not running out of food, but in getting sick. Savoonga then was without plumbing; water was carried from a central well in the village, and waste was collected in a honey bucket from each home. Having somewhat of a weak stomach, I felt sure I would get dysentery from my diet (a lot of whale meat, seal oil, and a variety of seabirds) but I didn't.

After a few weeks of living in the village and eating local foods, I was invited to go out with some young men to hunt seabirds, primarily murres. I excitedly accepted and found myself an hour or so later hiding behind an ice ridge while the hunters fired away when birds came within shotgun range. We had motored out along a series of leads away from the island and were on a large floe surrounded by a rapidly thawing Bering Sea. After a while I was getting cold just sitting and had noticed a bird fall some distance behind the hunters and no one else had seemed to notice so I decided to retrieve it. I got about halfway to the bird when the floor fell out from under me. I caught myself from going totally under by instinctively throwing my arms out to the side and falling forward. The ice broke a bit in front of me and then held. I was able to push and crawl back up out of the water. Unlike on the trapline, when the water never seemed to reach my skin, this time it did. I began to shiver almost at once. I had brought some extra clothing—a vest, woolen hat, gloves, and raincoat, and quickly set about pulling off what wet clothing I could easily replace. I was noticed about this time by a couple of the young hunters who giggled but kept on doing what they were doing. Perhaps this sort of thing was common, or perhaps they just thought I was a fool. I thought maybe a little of both were true.

Saving government quarter's roof from high winds – Cold Bay, Alaska.

David Wiswar – Winter fish studies, Arctic National Wildlife Refuge.

Chapter Seven:
SKY KING

Other than the methodical noise of my paddling and a prolonged "whoosh" from an occasional gust of wind, the whole of the surrounding environment was normally devoid of any sound. This was not only peaceful, but also set the stage for any interruption to the norm, like the alarm splash from a beaver's tail or the distant cry of a yellowlegs or mournful yodel of a loon. It had been days since I had heard a human voice and that had been from a short exchange with a fisherman tending his fish wheel as I floated by. The silence, only interrupted by natural sounds, is one of the most valued aspects of wilderness to me and such places are increasingly difficult to find in today's world. As I pondered this, a distant rumble became evident and steadily increased in the minutes to follow. "De Havilland Beaver," I said quietly to myself, one of the historic workhorse bush transport planes in Alaska, and easy to identify at a distance by the sound of its Pratt & Whitney engine and its nine cylinders pounding away. The noise brought back many memories and I was not disturbed by its presence. Bush planes are as much a part of Alaska as sled dogs, moose, and long underwear.

My introduction to bush plane travel illustrates how ignorant I was to their use and nomenclature when arriving in the North many years ago. Come late fall in 1979, I had been in Alaska for one year. This was a milestone because under State law, I was now considered a resident and could buy a hunting and fishing license for next to nothing. I couldn't wait to utilize my new status to attempt to put some meat in the freezer and set about researching the options. It was early December before the arrangements had been made. I was to fly to King Salmon with coworker Ron Stanek and call the air taxi operator to come get us—he was located a short distance away in Naknek. After landing and getting our gear, I made the call. I was instructed to go out front and look for a Cherokee in about 15 minutes. We waited an hour and then went back into the airport terminal and called again. The pilot said he had waited for 45 minutes and then left. After a brief discourse we discovered that I had been looking for a Jeep Cherokee out in the parking area while the pilot had been waiting in a Piper Cherokee on the tarmac. There were several other lessons learned on that trip also, mostly that tent camping was not much fun in December. We were both successful in getting caribou; however, Ron had to borrow my rifle to collect his because his rifle wouldn't fire in the cold temperatures. With only a few hours of daylight that time of year, we also couldn't make it back to our camp after getting our animals before it got dark and thus spent a VERY long night huddled together in a patch of alders trying to cook strips of caribou meat over a small smoky fire. And then it started to snow—a lot. Within a few hours we had two feet of accumulated snow. We made it back to our tent the next day and spent three days in our sleeping bags waiting for the weather to change and allow the plane to return and get us. A successful hunting adventure yes—fun, no.

Over the years to follow I spent hundreds of hours in bush planes in Alaska. I flew with some great pilots and some that made me want to kiss the ground after landing. One time I was flying with a well-known bush pilot, along the Arctic coastline and low under a fog bank, when I glanced over and found him fast asleep. I shook him awake and he murmured a thanks and nothing more was said. That was one of the times I looked longingly at the dirt with puckered lips as the plane's wheels touched down.

There is a saying in Alaska that there are old pilots, and bold pilots, but no old, bold pilots. There is more truth to that than not. The best pilot I ever flew with might have been an exception, if one could call Rod King old.

Rod was a pilot-biologist for the Migratory Birds Program (and the fellow who found Glenn Elison and me after we were overdue on a rafting trip that I described earlier). He flew more hours than any other pilot working for FWS that I knew of, mostly because he undertook extensive waterfowl surveys, not only across Alaska, but also some in Canada. Most surveys required long flights over remote areas and precisely flying repeatable transects crisscrossing the best waterfowl breeding habitats—places like the Yukon Flats. Some of us called Rod "Sky King" after the 1950's TV personality we remembered when growing up—reruns were aired on Saturdays right after "My Friend Flicka" ... Rod had names for most of his friends too, and just hearing him come into a room would bring a smile to your face. He was a bit irreverent and sometimes had disparaging remarks about the bureaucracy that employed him, but he was a good biologist and a heck of a pilot.

Rod had the boldness necessary to strike out for weeks at a time into remote terrain to undertake his work, but also the wisdom and experience to know when to temporarily suspend a mission. Once flying through a Brooks Range pass that was rapidly closing in around us with thick clouds, Rod suddenly dropped down out of the sky and landed on a small lake to wait out the weather. He knew the area well and planned for contingencies before committing to a course of action. Another time Rod sunk the floats on his Piper Cub so that the increasingly angry wind and waves on an Alaskan Range lake would not toss the light aircraft against the shore and damage it. After waiting out the storm he pumped the floats free of water and took off like nothing had happened.

My favorite account of flying with Rod was in August 1981. We were in an amphibious Beaver and after fueling at Umiat we did some sampling along the Colville River for the BLM and then hopped over to Teshekpuk Lake to spend the night. After securing the airplane and pitching our dome tent, Rod also tied another rope to the plane and ran it through a port hole in the tent where he then tied it around his chest before crawling into his sleeping bag. I remember giving him a bad time about that, but Teshekpuk

Lake is over 20 miles wide—too far to walk around looking for our transportation should the wind shift during the night. The wind did shift, and after a couple of gusts, Rod was jerked violently and we both scrambled out of the comfort of our sleeping bags into darkness and 15 degree temperatures to re-secure the aircraft.

I have other fond memories of Rod including our trip to Hawaii with fellow biologist and pilot Mike Smith in January 1982. That trip was the impetus for a traditional pig roast to be hosted at Rod's house every spring for many years. The trip was also when I came closest to ever succumbing to hypothermia. I found myself camping, but poorly equipped, high up on a mountain about nine miles into Haleakala National Park. As it rained, and blew, and started to snow, I shivered uncontrollably and thought of the potential headlines: "Alaskan biologist dies of exposure in Hawaii." Rod and Mike apparently had better gear and snored away while I learned an important lesson: latitude isn't as important as altitude.

To my knowledge Rod was involved in only one serious aircraft incident in his long career. Shortly after taking off in a Piper Cub from Bethel, the aircraft stalled and went down. Chris Dau was in front and Rod was in back. The accident was caused by a mechanical failure and was no fault of Rod or Chris, but both were affected for years to come. Rod required major dental reconstruction and Chris suffered a significant leg injury. Chris went on to be a great pilot in his own right, first as a pilot/biologist for Izembek and then for Migratory Birds.

Sadly, Rod passed away on Christmas Eve 2018. His legacy as a pilot-biologist was exceptional however and he was inducted as a "Conservation Hero" at the FWS training center (NCTC) in November 2019. He contributed more to waterfowl conservation than will ever be known, but he will never be forgotten and he will be forever missed.

FLYING WITH MIKE

I mentioned Mike Smith briefly above when recounting a 1982 trip to Hawaii. Mike for a time was a coworker, for a time my boss, for a time a pilot, and always my friend. We spent a lot of time in a fixed-wing airplane together for both work and pleasure. Mike was piloting the Cesena 206 (tracking radio-tagged northern pike and burbot on Tetlin National Wildlife Refuge) when I first learned that I could throw up while flying. I often got a little woozy but on this particular day we had just filled our bellies with blueberry pie in Northway and had begun extensive flying, snaking in and around river bends trying to fly precisely over all portions of the streams below with Mike at the helm and me with maps, notebook and pencil, a Telonics receiver in my lap, and earphones over my ears. The many turns of the Cessna were complemented by rapid and unpredictable bumps and drops in the aircraft as it responded to the warm afternoon thermals. About an hour into our searching for tagged fish, I knew the blueberry pie was trying to reappear. I had not prepared for such an event and though I was able to grab a garbage bag from my daypack before too big a mess ensued, I was never the same. Once I knew I could Ralph, "he" visited more frequently on future flights. I did prepare by carrying a good supply of barf bags on future surveys. I did not however, eat a piece of blueberry pie for at least 10 years.

Another fish-finding flight experience with Mike is worth some mention. We had been doing several years of work in the Arctic National Wildlife Refuge "1002 area" completing work generally mandated by Congress to theoretically help steer future decisions about oil and gas development. While public interest in potential impacts to the area's natural resources most often focused on impacts to caribou, muskoxen, and polar bears, the region's fisheries could also be negatively affected from some development activities. Most notable were the risks to limited freshwater overwintering sites. Oil exploration activities largely occurred in winter with the aid of ice roads (travel in summer required more permanent roads with enough gravel placed to buffer the underlying permafrost and avoid melting). To make ice roads, lots of water was needed and saltwater killed tundra vegetation after it melted. Arctic rivers are generally braided and shallow, and the few places that had deep pools and/or spring activity were the only readily available places to pump freshwater. They were also the places where fish could congregate and survive the long winter. Our mission was to map these sites and to do so we put transmitters in fish and followed them to their wintering areas.

Our first efforts at tagging Arctic fish were directed at Arctic char. Large numbers of these fish would migrate from glacially fed streams into the lagoons along the Beaufort Sea coast where they would fatten up on amphipods and mysids in summer before returning to freshwater wintering areas. Tagging and tracking them was relatively easy as the fish were fairly large and fed little while migrating, allowing us to use little finger–sized sealed transmitters and esophageal implants that researchers had already perfected on salmon. When we switched gears and started to look at Arctic grayling, we were on our own. These fish were much smaller, fed continuously until winter, and were a fairly delicate species. We pioneered tracking techniques using experimental small transmitters surgically implanted in the fish's body cavity.

With nearly 70 grayling hopefully "on the air," Mike and I were flying a tracking flight in winter in the Arctic and were hopeful to learn great things. Our focus that day was on the lower reaches of Itkilyariak Creek where we had tagged quite a number of grayling. Hearing no tell-tale "beeps" after repeatedly flying over the area caused no immediate concern. The stream was shallow and most certainly was frozen to the bottom at this point—we expected the fish to be elsewhere. We searched the most obvious locations: the nearby area influenced by Sadlerochit Springs, and the headwaters of the drainage at Peters and Schrader Lakes. Nada. We were now a bit concerned. Was all of our earlier work tagging the grayling for naught? We knew that the surgeries could have been too much for our patients and they may have died and washed downstream to saltwater where any signal would dissipate and not allow detection. We knew too that the new miniature transmitters that we were using had small batteries that could have failed too quickly in the cold water environment. Running out of possibilities I asked Mike how much fuel we had and after he assured we had enough we struck out for the Hulahula River which possessed some known "fish holes" that overwintered fish. Eureka! We located one fish and then another and then several more. During the life of the study we did find overwintering fish near Sadlerochit Springs, and in Peters and Schrader Lakes, but the movements discovered to the Hulahula River were the first evidence that Arctic grayling would migrate outside of a particular river system, and in this case, through the saline water of the Beaufort Sea as they moved from one river system to another. The work was published in the *Transactions of the American Fisheries Society* in 1992.

While Mike and I spent many hours together in a government-owned aircraft while working, we spent far more time together in his personal Cessna 170B. It was a basic aircraft, fitted with wheels in summer and wood skis in winter, and it served us well, though it required a lot of distance for a safe takeoff and that limited off runway landing opportunities considerably. We used it one winter to trap in the Kantishna area, about an hour's flight southwest of Fairbanks, and after many such trips, I had studied Mike's takeoff and landing sequence enough that I told him I thought I could bring us home if he ever was unable to fly. He laughed and said, "Please don't." I'm not disappointed that I never got the opportunity to try.

We did have a few adventures while trapping however. The tiny cabin we spent the night in was heated by a sheet metal "sheepherders" stove that we had bought new for less than $40. Within minutes of firing it up, we would transition from freezing to sweating. An hour or two after going to bed, however, the temperature in the cabin would be the same as outside. I remember sleeping in two down sleeping bags while wearing a union suit, down vest, down booties, gloves, and a heavy wool hat. We would have a pile of tinder and kindling next to the bunk so as to be able to reach over and load the stove and get it started before crawling from the downy cocoon. One particularly cold morning we had loaded the plane and were preparing to depart but couldn't get it started. The small single-burner Coleman stove beneath the covered cowling did not emit enough heat to warm the oil and allow the engine to turn over. No problem—we temporarily removed the wood stove from the cabin and outfitted it to heat the engine and after about 10 minutes were good to go.

Another cold day returning from the trapline was on a Super Bowl Sunday. Ground temperature was 42 degrees below zero, but at altitude, it was much colder. Other than being cold, the flying was perfect—calm, sunny, and clear blue sky—until we got back to Fairbanks. An inversion there had caused thick ice fog conditions and the International Airport, and its adjacent ski strip, were closed. We had to divert to the Chena Marina and land on a much shorter and unfamiliar marked-off area. We came in a little steep and super-cooled the engine, landing roughly with a "dead stick." While no damage was done to the plane or us, we were now a few miles from our parked vehicles and hoping to still catch the big game. After knocking on a couple of doors, we were able to make a call and get picked up, arriving at the office Super Bowl party before the chili was served. After the game we were taken to the airport to get our vehicles, but they wouldn't start anyway.

When I think of flying in Alaska, I think most of Ted Stevens. This is not because the Anchorage International Airport is named for the late senator, rather, it is because of how he lived on and ultimately left this earth. From where I sat for thirty years, I can think of no person who did more for Alaska that Senator Stevens. He was smart, dedicated, and no-nonsense. No matter that his career late in life was tainted by accused ethics violations—those who knew the man knew he was honorable, and unrelated to politics; the man also knew aviation and its hazards well.

Stevens served his country flying support missions for the Flying Tigers in WWII, earning the Distinguished Flying Cross; he flew back and forth from Alaska to Washington, D.C. likely more than any other person, as he served Alaska in the U.S. Senate from 1968 to 2009; and though seriously injured, he survived a Lear Jet crash in Anchorage in December 1978 when returning from a swearing-in ceremony for Governor Jay Hammond—the crash killed the Senator's first wife, Ann, as well as four others.

The last time I spoke with Senator Stevens was over lunch in Soldotna and he had just returned from a fishing trip in southwest Alaska. I asked him how it went and he said good, but that he had trouble with his balance while navigating slippery rocks and that such failings would likely lead to his ultimate demise. He feared he was losing his equilibrium, would stop being active, and that this would be the underlying cause of his end. Approximately two years later Ted died, along with four of the other nine passengers when their plane, an amphibious Otter, crashed near Aleknagik. He was on a fishing trip. At 86 he had lived a full life—a fearless life, though brushing the edge of death repeatedly in an aluminum tube sailing across the sky, he did not alter course. I have great respect for the man. When it is your time to go, it is your time to go. Flying is still one of the safest means of transportation available, and in Alaska, it frequently is the only practical way available. You fly or you stay home.

Rod "Sky" King – Teshekpuk Lake – NPR-A.

Chris Dau – Izembek National Wildlife Refuge.

Chapter Eight:
EGGS, BIRDS, AND TREATIES

The Yukon Flats region is known for its waterfowl nesting habitat and this was the primary reason 8.63 million acres of it was set aside under ANILCA as a national wildlife refuge. Ducks, geese, swans, cranes, loons, and grebes come to the area to nest by the hundreds of thousands. The Flats drain approximately 300 miles of the Yukon River, and its broad plain supports about 20,000 lakes, ponds, and wetland complexes. Waterfowl banded there have been recovered from at least 45 states and 11 foreign countries.

Management of the Yukon Flats focuses on waterfowl of course, but ANILCA required attention be given to all fish and wildlife species and today's programs demonstrate that diversity. When I was the Assistant Manager, there in the late 1980s we did our waterfowl surveys, but also undertook fisheries' research and worked to recover depleted moose populations. Additional work addressed furbearers, botany, invertebrates, and the effects of fire. Along with conducting biological work we worked with the villages on subsistence issues and managed special use permits for a variety of activities. The one I remember most was Exxon's seismic exploration program. The Refuge was without roads, and access to any village lands from the Dalton Highway required crossing large expanses of undeveloped refuge. Seismic programs in Alaska at the time all employed dozing wide trails and pulling cat trains along the lines in winter to support the operation. This damaged vegetation and soils and left scars on the land that could last a century. Such seismic trails were not just eyesores. They could expose permafrost, become erosion gullies, and act as conduits for invasive plants. We were able to get Exxon to employ the Poulter technique that had been used somewhat in Canada. It utilized helicopter transport and charges on stakes above ground rather than placed in drilled holes. When done, the subsurface oil potential had been mapped on the targeted Native lands and the Refuge was left without any sign that the work had ever occurred. I felt pretty good about that.

The fact that the area is one of the greatest waterfowl production areas in the world is not disputed now, but it was almost lost to a proposed hydroelectric project, originally proposed in 1954, but clung to life for years to follow. The project would have dammed the Yukon just downstream of the current refuge boundary at Rampart Canyon and created a reservoir approaching the size of Lake Eerie. No matter that the seven small villages in the Region had no interest in such a project, or that it would have destroyed forever the area's productive wetlands, the project was a brainchild of the Army Corp of Engineers and at the time the feds were still managing Alaska with little environmental oversight legislatively or procedurally. The project grew in favor in some circles as the United States elevated discussions over energy needs generally, and voiced specific concern about falling behind the Soviet Union in technology. Though not directly related to development of hydroelectric projects and the like, national attention on the Russians being ahead in the race to space, by successfully launching sputnik, spilled over into discussions of many large projects under consideration. It was voices of people like FWS biologist Jim King, a migratory bird biologist-pilot like Rod King, but from the previous generation, that were most involved in saving the Flats. Having knowledge of the area's extreme importance to waterfowl production, and a willingness to speak up, biologists like Jim were able to beat down the proposal. Such expertise and voices were not limited to advocacy against the Rampart Dam and other projects, but were also invaluable in developing the maps and arguments used ultimately to protect many important waterfowl conservation areas in the State as ANILCA legislation was formulated. Input from seasoned FWS employees like Jim, Cal Lensink, and Bill Refault brought credibility to the size and location of proposed new refuges. Of course politics and a little agency tribalism influenced the fate of some of their proposals. In the end not all of their recommended areas became refuges but for those that did, they included some of the best of the best in support of waterfowl conservation.

Generally most Alaska refuges are thought of as waterfowl nesting areas, and it is true that some of the best places in the world that support nesting waterfowl are found in Alaska, the Yukon Delta National Wildlife Refuge (at 19.16 million acres) and the Yukon Flats NWR included. Alaska refuges also provide important wintering habitat for seabirds and waterfowl, especially along the shores of the 2,400 islands, rocks, and headlands within the 4.9 million acre Alaska Maritime National Wildlife Refuge. At Izembek NWR, there is minimal waterfowl nesting, some important overwintering, but the most significant value of the 300,000 acres is the large eelgrass lagoon that provides critical staging habitat for waterfowl, especially black brant. The brant feed on the eelgrass for approximately two months in the fall and then most fly continuously for 48 hours to wintering grounds, primarily in Baja, Mexico. They can lose up to a third of their body weight in this flight—if they have not fattened up enough at Izembek, they literally fall out of the air en route. The National Wildlife Refuge System works to conserve habitats that provide for all life history functions of waterfowl and other species. If one important link is lost, the investments made elsewhere can be for naught.

Earlier in my career, while serving as the FWS migratory bird coordinator for the Alaska FWS Region, I was repeatedly reminded how important the Flats was to waterfowl production for North America, particularly in times of draught in the pothole region of Lower 48 prairie states. As time passed too, I saw more wetlands in the Lower 48 drained and grasslands of the Dakotas converted to corn production. In the long run, protecting areas like the Flats, and its expansive and pristine watery ecosystem, will likely make the difference between some waterfowl species surviving in good numbers versus becoming rare or worse.

AMENDING A TREATY

My job as the migratory bird coordinator would have normally been directed at waterfowl surveys, banding programs, research, and participation in annual regulation-setting processes. This I did, but an important part of the position during my tenure was helping to bring about changes to subsistence hunting of migratory birds. Conflicts were growing over a legal problem yet to be resolved, although earlier attempts had been made. At issue was the restrictions in the 1916 Migratory Bird Treaty with Great Britain (on the behalf of Canada), it's implementing law—the Migratory Bird Treaty Act of 1918 (MBTA), and the prohibitions that made spring hunting and egg gathering illegal, no matter the practice's history or how noble its cause might be. This put the traditional practices of thousands of indigenous people in Alaska and Canada at odds with the law. It also essentially guaranteed that wildlife managers could expect little if any cooperation from Native people when trying to collect harvest information and/or implement specific restrictions to conserve certain species that required additional protection. After all, who wants to work with the government, by in so doing, you implicate yourself to breaking laws that the same government is mandated to enforce?

Understanding the origin of the MBTA helps to put into perspective how earlier actions set the stage for later problem. Early in the 20th century, migratory bird populations were in serious trouble. Unregulated market hunting for food and a growing demand for plumes and feathers, particularly for women's hats, were fueling the decimation of many bird populations, particularly in the eastern United States and Canada. A call for action resulted in the signing of the 1916 treaty, 1918 law, and specific regulations designed to limit take to certain bird species and to certain times of the year. This was done with only minor discussion of issues not central to the urgent need for bird conservation. Alaska was far away and it was a few years later before formal attention was given to its unique conservation challenges when the Alaska Game Act of 1925 was passed. Subsequent treaties were signed to conserve what was becoming increasingly acknowledged as an internationally shared migratory bird resource—with Mexico in 1936, Japan in 1972, and the Soviet Union in 1976, and amendments were made to the MBTA. The federal assertion to regulate take of migratory birds (over that of individual states) was not without challenges but the issue was settled rather quickly in the landmark case *Missouri* v. *Holland* (1920). The Supreme Court held that the federal government was justified to reach out to protect migratory birds as a food resource, and the treaty-making powers and Supremacy Clause of the U.S. Constitution granted them the authority to do so. The treaties following the 1916 initial agreement came with growing awareness of the subsistence hunting conundrum and ultimately would require little to no amendments—the restrictions imposed by the 1916 Convention, however, were always going to be problematic if not changed.

Two particular events in Alaska history especially evidenced the need to amend the 1916 Canadian Treaty. The first was the Barrow "Duck-In." Although Project Chariot took most of the headlines in the news of 1961 in northern Alaska, a public protest at Point Barrow in May of that year also garnered notable national attention. (Project Chariot was another federal brainchild project, like Rampart Dam, only this one proposed to blast a deep water harbor near Point Hope using an atomic device.)

The Barrow incident grew from the arrest of a local hunter for taking a duck out of season; it resulted in a group of 138 men, women, and children presenting 138 ducks to the warden, also asking to be arrested. While other less reported enforcement actions were also undertaken by State enforcement officers in rural areas early after statehood, it was a federal law they were enforcing so it was a federal problem. And whether a federal or state officer, all were aware that people in remote areas of Alaska had for thousands of years taken migratory birds in the spring, often followed by their eggs; these were a dependable and important protein source for rural residents before salmon started migrating up local rivers. The need for food in the more remote areas remained paramount, and the traditional practice itself was unlikely to be abandoned even if alternative food sources became available, especially if it only meant saving the birds so they could be shot later by hunters in the Lower 48.

The second historical event of note in addressing subsistence take of birds and eggs during the closed season was much more drawn out. Surveys demonstrated that severe declines in four species of Arctic nesting geese, reaching levels of concern before the early 1980s, required special management attention. Three of the declining species (black brant, Pacific white-fronted geese, and cackling Canada geese) were shared between Alaska and the Lower 48 Pacific Flyway states, primarily California. The third declining species, the emperor goose, never left Alaska, except for a few that moved back and forth from the Aleutian Islands or the Yukon–Kuskokwim Delta and the Soviet Union. It took a few years of finger-pointing by user groups before managers could get down to business. Hunters in the Lower 48 blamed the Natives in Alaska and held that if they didn't kill the birds before they nested, there wouldn't be a problem. Alaska Natives felt that their subsistence use of the birds was more important than any take by sport hunters and that if any group should curtail their use, it should be Lower 48 hunters. Eventually, and with some effort, including trips that took Native Alaska hunters to California, and vice versa, tensions generally softened. Both groups realized how important the hunting was to the other and that they both cared about waterfowl conservation and the preservation of future harvest opportunities. From a practical point, however, regulatory changes and enforcement was much easier to undertake in the south. Up north, most of the harvest was already illegal, but wasn't going to stop anytime soon, and enforcement was largely impractical over large remote landscapes, and could sometimes even prove counterproductive as well.

To address the legitimate need of many Native Alaskans to continue to take migratory birds for food in the spring, but to also try and minimize the take of species of conservation concern, an agreement was reached in

1984. The Hooper Bay Agreement (named after one of the villages on the Yukon–Kuskokwim Delta involved in the negotiations) and the agreement's successor the following year, the Yukon–Kuskokwim Goose Management Plan, both permitted some take of common waterfowl species and restricted the take of species of conservation concern. Both agreements were struck down after legal challenge, finding that FWS had no authority to allow spring take of migratory birds that was otherwise prohibited by treaty and the MBTA. The court provided an out for FWS however, allowing that while the Agency couldn't legitimize actions that were legally prohibited, it could set priorities for enforcement. FWS quickly took this approach and the Goose Management Plan was redrafted. This marked the beginning of the FWS discretionary law enforcement policy that addressed spring hunting of migratory birds in Alaska. In essence, subsistence hunters were informed that the highest priorities for enforcement were three things: (1) the take of the four species of geese or their eggs (spectacled and Steller's eiders were also added later to the "prohibited list"), (2) the use of aircraft in support of hunting birds in the spring, and (3) wanton waste of birds or eggs (any species). It was understood, but not in print as a regulation, that all other take of migratory birds for subsistence purposes would likely see no enforcement action. Formalization of the new policy, and communicating it widely, began in earnest about the time I entered the MBTA amendment arena.

Earlier attempts to amend the MBTA had largely failed due to lack of will by some powers to be, or even subliminal actions by various groups and individuals that had connections to decision-makers. Fundamentally it was clear that Alaska Natives had just as much right to kill and eat a duck or goose as a hunting club member in California or a farmer in Oregon. It was also a biological fact that killing a female duck or goose in the spring meant less of the species would be available overall compared to inflicting the mortality after brood rearing—the very reason for the spring hunting restrictions in the first place. Some seemed to hope the issue would just fade away. Others seemed fine with a perpetual use of the FWS discretionary enforcement policy. Native leaders in Alaska would have none of that. They had waited long enough watching as people were made out as criminals for just feeding their families in the fashion undertaken for generations. Equally important, Canada was unwilling to maintain the status quo indefinitely. Recent legal review in their country determined that take of fish and wildlife by their First Nations people was a constitutional right, akin to our freedom of speech or right to bear arms. While all hunting and fishing opportunities in the United States (unless preserved specifically by treaty) are privileges, not rights, and can be restricted by law, this was not so for Native peoples in Canada. Ultimately it was this fact that helped move the needle on the issue. Fear that Canada might be forced to abrogate the 1916 Treaty, resulting in its renegotiation and a potentially different allocation of a shared resource, lead the way for many of the groups in the United States that had opposed any legalization of spring subsistence hunting to reconsider their position.

During this time I traveled a great deal—to Washington, D.C., Canada, various states, and to many Alaskan villages. I was gone more than not—one of my young children thought I lived at the airport, another that I somehow lived in the telephone. I met with village leaders, representatives with the State Department, Canadian Embassy officials, sportsmen's groups, State wildlife agencies, conservation organizations, and elected officials. After several years of work, an Alaskan Native working group was formed and we collectively began drafting a protocol to amend the treaty. The Canadian Wildlife Service was undergoing similar discussions and we met regularly to compare notes.

Besides the growing need to address Canada's constitutional concerns, another factor that facilitated advancing the proposed treaty amendments more favorably this time around, was the staff dedicated to the work. Mollie Beatty was the FWS Director and once the groundwork had been set, she employed a seasoned negotiator, Buff Bohlen, to lead our team. Dave Allen was a supportive Regional Director in Alaska; my direct supervisor, Dr. John Rogers, was a veteran of previous treaty amendment attempt battles, and a former Chief of the Migratory Birds Office (MBO) in Washington, D.C.—he had the background knowledge and support for the effort and the respect of Native leaders. The current Chief of MBO was Paul Schmidt, John's previous deputy in Alaska, and well versed in the issue and motivated to see it resolved. He had staff support by Keith Morehouse who provided a steady hand in coordinating meetings, drafting documents, and ensuring public involvement was undertaken. With growing national support and many talented hands helping, the seemingly easy remedy to tweak the 1916 Treaty to include a managed spring hunt for subsistence purposes was still far from done. Different Alaska Native villages wanted specific assurances, and protests in Canada stemmed from some First Nations people also feeling they were being left out of decisions that would affect their future. The State of Alaska Administration had also changed and their position shifted, including the desire to have eligibility for the spring hunt go to qualified rural residents (regardless of race) - similar to the subsistence provisions in Title VIII of ANILCA vs. hunting privileges restricted only to Alaska Natives - similar to the provisions of the Marine Mammals Protection Act. A core promise to non-governmental conservation groups, who were watching the proposed amendments with interest, was that a new legalized hunt would not mean more dead birds—no new opportunity, only a recognition and cooperative management of take that was already occurring. As various changes and concessions were being discussed, biological considerations were evaluated and ultimately had to shape any final proposal.

In the spring of 1995, the Canadian and U.S. delegations met at Nanaimo, British Columbia, and hammered out a final agreement to amend the 1916 Treaty. The Protocol to amend the treaty was signed later in December of 1995 and transmitted to the Senate by President Clinton on August 2, 1996. The Senate approved the amendments, along with minor amendments to the treaty with Mexico, in 1997. In several years following, implementation began to take place. An Alaskan Migratory Bird Co-Management Council was created to consist of equal partnerships between FWS, ADF&G, and representatives from Alaska Native communities. The co-management group works through the FWS regulations setting process, like states and flyway councils, to set regulations based on public input and steered by biological data and management plan goals and objectives. Today's regulations recognize a legal traditional spring harvest and set dates for when the harvest can occur, limit methods and means of the take and what species may be harvested, and details where in Alaska the hunting can take place and by whom. I suspect no one would argue that the end result is a perfect one, but it seems fair, and certainly is a vast improvement over ignoring the problem, enforcing an unjust law, or debating how to enforce part of the law part of the time. It also is a good reminder how much easier it is generally to do most things right the first time rather than trying to work a fix down the road. Change, of any kind, is generally hard.

GETTING THE LEAD OUT

Another management challenge with migratory birds in Alaska was implementing new regulations that limited waterfowl hunting to only the use of non-toxic shot in shotgun ammunition. Scientists had known for years that lead shot was toxic if ingested by birds and that waterfowl were particularly susceptible. Spent lead pellets from years of hunting over wetlands were periodically picked up by feeding ducks, presumably as grit to aid in grinding of seeds and vegetation in their gizzards. The grinding broke down the lead pellets too and the lead was absorbed through the digestive tract and into the bloodstream. Even one pellet could result in death to a bird and some estimates suggested over a million ducks could be succumbing to lead poisoning each year.

Though the science was sound and the problem fairly well understood, advocates from the shooting community, and waterfowl hunters in particular, were not keen on losing the opportunity to use lead ammunition to hunt. Fears over guns being ruined from shooting (harder) steel shot, or even blowing up, wounding of birds from what was believed to be a less effective pellet material, and the increased cost of non-lead ammunition, all contributed to delays in the inevitable eventuality that lead shot would be banned. Change, of any kind, is generally hard.

The timing of the switch to non-toxic shot was ultimately driven by toxicity to eagles rather than ducks. Bald eagles were protected by the Endangered Species Act and numerous cases documented eagles dying from eating ducks that had died or were dying from lead poisoning. Litigation forced change and the use of lead shotgun ammunition for hunting waterfowl was phased out starting in the 1987–1988 hunting season—the first areas affected were those with the biggest problems and the most hunters—lead shot for waterfowl hunting was prohibited nationwide, including Alaska, by 1991. Steel was the only real alternative to lead in the early days, though several other approved non-toxic shot options exist today.

With increased availability, steel shot became more affordable. Studies were undertaken and information disseminated to help hunters make the transition and ease concern over the effectiveness of steel. In general, hunters were advised to use a larger pellet size (so that the lighter steel projectiles would retain similar amounts of energy downrange as lead) and to use a more open choke (to allow the harder steel pellets that didn't deform upon firing, and spread out, to provide a similar pattern as lead). Steel ammunition was also loaded with protective plastic wads that encased the shot column as it passed through the shotgun barrel, preventing damage. The improvements were all good, but resistance to the change was still high in some areas. Education and enforcement were employed and compliance improved. In Alaska, however, compliance in rural areas initially was non-existent. The biggest factor was village stores were still carrying lead ammunition (which was still legal for hunting upland game in most of North America, and it was cheaper). Hunters used what was available and few probably knew about the legal changes, or if they did, were probably not overly concerned. At that time, most of the waterfowl hunting they were doing was still illegal anyway.

The impetus to step up compliance with the use of non-toxic shot in Alaska came after the listing of the spectacled eider as a threatened species.

Jim King, shortly after retirement from FWS, once again used his knowledge and voice to positively affect change for waterfowl conservation by filing a petition to list both spectacled and Steller's eiders for protection under the Endangered Species Act. As an active employee such action would have undoubtedly been frowned upon—listing a species that our agency had primary management responsibilities for kind of admitted failure and could be viewed as an embarrassment. In truth, the two eiders had fallen through the cracks. Most visitors to Alaska never saw these species and most sport hunters engaged in the fall waterfowl season never harvested one. Nonetheless, FWS's own data indicated that spectacled eiders had experienced over an 80 percent decline in recent years, and no one knew why. The case for Steller's eiders was less compelling. While historic data indicated some nesting of Steller's eiders near Barrow and on the Yukon–Kuskokwim Delta in years past (and later was nearly absent), it was generally believed that Alaska was on the fringe of the nesting range for this species, and that most production occurred in the Soviet Union. Tens of thousands of the species did winter in Alaska, in Izembek Lagoon or near Kodiak Island, but nesting was rare. An initial decision was made to list the spectacled eider as a threatened species and to do nothing immediately regarding Steller's eiders. A common practice at the time was making a finding that a species was likely warranted for listing but it was precluded by higher priorities (given limited funding). Within a year or so, settlement of a lawsuit that addressed a number of "warranted but precluded" species nationwide, resulted in the addition of the Alaska population of Steller's eiders to the threatened species list. It then joined the (range-wide) protection of spectacled eiders. Now FWS needed to find out why these birds were declining and what could be done to reverse it.

Many theories were discussed on why the spectacled eider population had so rapidly and significantly declined. Some believed that they were the next largest target of choice in the spring for hunters that would have previously preferred to take one of the declining Arctic nesting goose species. Others felt predation could be a significant factor, also suggesting that declining Arctic nesting geese left fewer options for hungry foxes. Biologists understood that the eiders were different than other waterfowl species and due to their harsh environment, frequently had failed nesting attempts. It took longer for them to replace themselves, say compared to a mallard or pintail. Biologically this was taken care of as a rule because the species also were longer lived. The challenge for the species was, and always had been, to ensure they lived long enough to have offspring through future generations. One known mortality factor for waterfowl was lead poisoning. Initially this was thought to be an unlikely issue for Alaska, but studies early on proved otherwise. In the Yukon–Kuskokwim Delta area, the primary breeding grounds for spectacled eiders, a significant number of nesting hens sampled had elevated lead blood levels. Apparently the hunting activities from over 50 villages in the same general area for many decades had deposited enough lead in the wetlands to be a problem. There was little that could be done to remove the old spent pellets, but efforts could be undertaken to prevent the addition of any more. Future research also found previously undiscovered wintering grounds for the bulk of the spectacled eider population—grouped together in an open water lead in an otherwise frozen Bering Sea. Such a strategy could easily subject the population to a severe decline if even one large storm resulted in the birds being unable to feed for a prolonged time, or worse, have the lead freeze closed with no nearby alternatives for open water. This discovery might have best explained the likely decline in the eider numbers, but it did not lessen the concern over lead poisoning. Managers had to focus on things within their control to bring about the birds' recovery, and dictating the winter weather for the Bering Sea wasn't on the list.

I remember my first attempt to convince Native hunters that lead poisoning was a serious problem, and it that it could be remedied over time. I was in Bethel meeting with the Association of Village Council President's Waterfowl Conservation Committee. After my presentation was translated, an elder on the Committee began speaking while rolling up a sleeve exposing an old wound that had healed long ago but had also left some of the muscle clearly missing. He said, that has a boy, he had been involved in a hunting accident and that a shotgun had gone off while hunting birds and that he had been seriously injured. Some of the pellets were still in his damaged arm some 60 years later, but that he had healed fine. If he had been using steel shot, he shared, the pellets would have rusted and he would have died.

I listened carefully to the translation from Yupik to English, and knew that the rusty pellet concern was not true, but basically could say nothing out of respect. The meeting was over. A couple months later I was back for another go at it. There were good questions at the end of my presentation and I was hopeful that progress had been made, but the meeting ended similarly to the last one. This time I was told that, while lead poisoning could be an issue with white hunters, not so with the village hunters. I was informed that they were good shots and the pellets went into the bird, not missing and falling into the marsh. Again, I knew this to be untrue as even the best shot only strikes the target with a small percentage of the ammunition's payload, but could say nothing effectively to refute the claim.

Success on the issue was reached later somewhat by chance. I arranged to take a delegation of Alaska Native leaders to Illinois where Tom Roster was putting on steel shot shooting clinics with the support of the Winchester shot shell factory and the nearby NILO Farms. Tom had worked for a number of years testing steel shot loads for effectiveness and was the leading expert on non-toxic shot use and its performance. The clinics allowed participants to see how the ammunition was manufactured in the factory, how it worked via classroom presentations, and how it performed in the field. Participants got to shoot a lot of steel shots at clay targets but at the end of the class they also got to shoot pen-reared mallards under field conditions and then look at the harvested birds using x-ray, then finally through dissection. There was no apparent breakthrough until the very end when totally by chance one of the ducks shot by a Native hunter was being dissected by the group and it was discovered to have previously ingested a lead pellet. The bird had been killed cleanly by the steel ammunition, but that wasn't the take-home message. The duck was thin, its keel evident and breast muscles were wasting away. The bird had a dark-green stain on its vent and when the gizzard was opened, it exhibited a smelly green goo and a partially ground-away lead shotgun pellet. If a picture was worth a thousand words, a green gizzard was worth ten thousand. Those representatives went back to Alaska with a new perspective. Follow-up work with village leaders and local stores to stock the right size of steel shotgun ammunition, and steel shot clinics conducted by FWS and ADF&G employees in rural communities, resulted in a near complete turnaround in support and use of non-toxic shot throughout much of rural Alaska.

Chapter Nine:
MEAT FOR THE TABLE

While I had ample supplies of freeze-dried food, snacks, and other consumables stowed in waterproof bags on board, I hoped to supplement dinners with fresh fish. That really isn't as easy as it might seem. The Yukon River is teaming with a large variety of fish for sure, but catching them in the fast, silty water is more than challenging using conventional means. Locals rarely use hook and line to catch fish, and frankly, the concept of recreational fishing (at least when it means "catch and release") is foreign to them. Gill nets and current-driven fish wheels work well, however, and many villagers spend a portion of the summer months in traditional fish camps to gather a winter's supply—primarily king and chum salmon. For me, not being a qualified subsistence user, I was limited to rod and reel. To be successful, I had to fish clear-water tributaries, primarily for northern pike and Arctic grayling, or soak bait on the bottom in backwater sloughs (for burbot). On this trip I was most successful with pike, which grab almost any moving lure in their toothy mouth with aggression, but then resist little while they are being reeled in. The fight isn't important when fishing for food and actually less resistance is good to reduce the chance that your intended dinner escapes. Pike are boney and can be a little muddy tasting, though I like the flavor. The biggest issue for me was catching a small enough one as eating a larger fish by myself is kind of like eating half a fruit cake. The first dozen bites are great, but then obligation sets in and I didn't want to waste anything. In one case, after about two dozen bites, I was reminded that I should have let that one go and kept something smaller.

In modern times, the order of concern for survival in Alaska would probably be first to not get hypothermia and succumb to the elements, followed distantly by not being eaten by something large, like a bear, or small, like mosquitos. Undoubtedly these were concerns for Native people historically too, but by far the biggest threat to survival in times before European contact was not having an adequate and predictable food supply. Counter to some popular belief, wild game in Alaska can be scarce over large expanses of real estate for long periods of time. And even when dependable food sources were present, like migratory birds or migrating salmon, their availability was seasonal and preservation of large amounts was challenging. Then too, even the best efforts of caching dried fish, for example, could be ruined by a single visit from a marauding bear. It is little wonder then that subsistence hunting for bowhead whales by Inupiat and Yupik people has taken on a rich spiritual meaning in local culture. The successful take of one of these creatures could feed a whole village for more than a year—the meat and blubber kept frozen with the aid of underground permafrost. Larger "freezers" were accessed by ladders and creating them must have been quite an undertaking without modern tools, but once constructed they might be utilized regularly for hundreds of years. The justifiable concern over famine over thousands of years of history helps explain also a common theme of many Native subsistence users that when an animal presents itself to a hunter, it should be taken. To not do so is a personal affront to the Creator and the opportunity may be taken away if not accepted graciously. From a practical standpoint, such a belief system also helped stave off starvation. Take what you can when you can. You might need it later.

One of the reasons that I became a biologist in the first place, and eagerly went to Alaska when the opportunity presented itself, was my love for hunting and fishing. In my college years I was surrounded by like-minded classmates—primarily young men, almost all Caucasian, and nearly all having come from a rural upbringing. As time passed, the field of wildlife biology diversified greatly; people, regardless of gender, race, or background, were naturally drawn to the wonders of wild animals, and social change had supported a growing natural empathy for creatures over simply viewing them as a food source. I believe that this is a product of people becoming more urbanized throughout the world, but still following a silent call from the wild—relating with other living things with an innate connection to which they are inexplicitly drawn. These changes have sometimes been difficult for old-school biologists to accept, but I think overall they have been good. A diverse group of advocates for the wildlife resource may disagree on whether animals are best viewed as food, sport, subjects of art or study, or are worthy of consideration equal to humans, but different values matter little if there is agreement that wildlife are important and should be conserved. After all, you must have healthy wildlife populations now if you want to haggle over their value and uses later. In rural Alaska, however, there is little patience for those who believe animals should be protected over the needs of people. Alaska's Constitution in Article 8 (Sections 3 and 4) supported rural Alaska's view then and now in stating, "Whenever occurring in their natural state, fish, wildlife, and waters are reserved to the people for common use. Fish, forests, wildlife, grasslands, and all other replenishable resources belonging to the State shall be utilized, developed, and maintained on the sustained yield principle, subject to preference among beneficial uses." When I moved to Alaska in 1978 there was little debate over people's use of its resources, except for early signs of unrest regarding some predator control programs, and I fit in well. I had grown up harvesting and eating wild game, and looked forward to continuing the practice in the great land.

Why was I a hunter? I gave little thought to that question in my earliest years, being surrounded by friends and family with the same views and practices until I reached my late teens. I think I first asked the question of myself returning to Oregon from a successful elk hunt in Idaho. The large six-point antlers from the elk I had taken were tied on top off our stock truck, not so much out any interest in showing them off, but out of necessity given their size. When stopping to fuel the truck some people pulled in behind us and their disdain for what they saw was obvious. It was the first time I realized not everyone felt the same as I did about hunting. For me though, it was a way of life—I knew no other. I remember my mother cooking beef at home, other than hamburger, only two times growing up. We ate deer and elk, with an occasional antelope or bear.

Mom hunted some, but only I think to please Dad. Her mother, Elizabeth Candee, was from English stock, her ancestors arriving in the United States shortly after the Mayflower. Mom's great-grandfather, George Candee, was a preacher and abolitionist—a prolific writer who petitioned President Lincoln on the cause against slavery, but there was no evidence that he was ever a hunter. My Mom's father, John Dopyera, had immigrated from what is now Slovakia to Los Angeles in the 1920s. He told me once he remembered hunting hares in the old country but he was from a family of millers and cabinet makers. He himself was a noted inventor and maker of musical instruments, with his most famous invention being the DOBRO resonator guitar, but he was not a hunter. On my Dad's side there was a hunting history. His mother, Elizabeth Balch, had descended from Abenaki Indian and Irish ancestors on her father's side, and English and Scot on her mother's side. His father, Lester West, was a decedent of John West, a bridge builder who emigrated from Ireland around 1780. One might think that it was the American-Indian ancestry that triggered the hunting instinct in my family roots, but I think it was the Irish. The family history throughout over 100 years of early life in Vermont, and then in Nevada and Oregon, was filled with stories of hardworking large families that eked out a living from timbering, farming, and odd jobs, supplemented by what the land around them provided. Dad grew up the same way, and raised me to appreciate the land and what it offered as well. The take of wild animals for food was not only a way of life, it was a shared connection with family, now present and those already gone, and a connection to the land itself. I decided to make a career out of trying to preserve that way of life by ensuring fish and wildlife would remain abundant in a changing world—a world of more and more people, and with an increasing number of them possessing an increasing appetite for natural resources.

I have many fond memories of hunting and fishing growing up—my first deer, a particularly good day of steelhead fishing, extended treks into wilderness with friends and family, and enjoying many fine meals from nature's bounty. My strongest memory though is not a fond one. It was formed from a trip I was not even on. My sister and I were in our mid-teens and old enough to fend for ourselves. We had just started the school year at Grants Pass High School and our parents were off traveling with relatives from back East. Mom and two aunts were visiting Vancouver Island in British Columbia and Dad and two of his brothers were deer hunting in the backcountry of Idaho. Twenty-three miles from the trailhead, on opening day of hunting season, my uncle Charles was shot and killed. The hunter who pulled the trigger was no stranger to the woods. He had worked for many years as a logger and had hunted often; he had taken a cow elk the previous year from near the same location that he shot my uncle. Perhaps that memory of the elk, and thinking he would repeat it, contributed to his ill-fated decision to fire his rifle that September morning. It was a remote location, and it was unlikely the shooter and his companion were aware there were other hunters nearby. It was during pre-dawn hours—visibility was limited. The season opened for deer and elk that morning, and both sexes were legal, so no antlers had to be seen before firing. None of these conditions, however, justified the action. It was careless, unchangeable, and fatal. My uncle never saw the shot coming I am sure—he was likely facing the other way, resting from a steep climb on a sagebrush-covered slope above a small pack trail below. A single shot from a 30-06 rifle struck him through his red hat, killing him instantly. He certainly did not suffer, but plenty of other folks did. My father arrived on the scene shortly thereafter and worried over restraining his other brother from not doing something he would regret later. The shooter and his companion were greatly impacted too—who wouldn't be? The lasting effect of the accident impacted many families for years to come. For me, it changed my life. No longer did I have a carefree attitude when tromping around the woods. Hearing a gunshot would give me pause. Most notably, I would get anxious when daylight was fading and my father had not yet returned to camp. Those uncontrollable feelings did not prevent me from continuing to hunt, but they did temper my joy when doing so. They also contributed to my commitment to teach hunter safety to others—I was an instructor in Alaska for over 20 years. Even for those who did not hunt, or have any interest in learning, the firearm safety aspect of the course was valuable to all—young and old. There were few households in Alaska that did not contain at least one firearm, and nearly everyone would encounter weapons during their lives. Recognizing safe handling and use of firearms saves lives and it certainly is not learned from watching television or movies.

As our family grew in Alaska, our use of fish and wildlife as food increased proportionately. At peak demand (during the kids' teen years) we would eat approximately one moose, two caribou, or four deer each year. We would supplement this irregularly with other big game such as Dall sheep, mountain goat, and bear, as well as with fish and birds. Our favorite meat was from a buffalo I got one year near Delta Junction. Plains Bison are not native to Alaska but several populations were established many years ago and limited hunting opportunity is offered. Drawing a tag is the difficult part and the odds the year I got my bull were approximately 130:1. Alaska has quite a few limited draw opportunities for hunting of big game today, but historically, most hunting occurred during general seasons and without special permits.

I guess the second best tasting meat to me was mountain goat, though it was so tough when coming from an old billy that it generally had to be ground to be enjoyed. My least favorite was bear, though we had some good ones too. The only meat that seemed nearly inedible to me was older bull caribou taken in peak rut. I never did so, but knew others who tried this, usually just once. While a breeding bull caribou is a striking animal with a long white mane and dark polished antlers, its meat, during a short time of the year, holds a strong musky odor that overwhelms one when cooking, and hits the palate like spoiled cabbage when being consumed. I avoided hunting caribou in October, but other than that I had no complaints about any of the game meat the land offered.

I enjoyed all of the hunting, but most appreciated the alpine habitats of wild sheep and goats. Glaciers, colorful tundra, and crystal clear waterfalls are just some of the attributes that made visits to the high country most memorable. For the hunting itself, I most enjoyed stalking Sitka black-tailed deer. They were plentiful on Kodiak and adjacent islands and I could bone one out and remove its entire carcass on the day of harvest—always a plus when hunting in brown bear country. When I first started hunting deer in Alaska, the season was five months long, the bag limit was seven of either sex, and the tags (harvest tickets) were free (for residents). The deer were also numerous enough that I could pick my shots and still be nearly ensured of success on most trips when using my preferred weapon, a traditional bow.

After bison and mountain goat, the meat of choice was moose. It was lean and mild tasting. Moose were a lot of work though, and a thoughtful hunter would not shoot one too far from a dependable means of transportation—usually a raft, riverboat, or canoe—or where you could drive reasonably close with an ATV or highway vehicle, or land a bush plane. A moose would take six to ten backpack loads and that was difficult to accomplish quickly unless transportation was nearby. Here again the presence of bears was a factor, as could be the weather in earlier seasons. An ethical hunter did all they could to protect their harvest from loss to spoilage or scavengers. For one particular moose I took I had no such worries as it was in mid-December after all bears should be hibernating. The temperature was plenty cold also, at 26 degrees below zero; it was like hunting within a giant freezer. I remember rubbing the wood limbs on my bow before drawing and releasing the arrow, fearing the bow might shatter. It didn't, and the bull was only on its feet for a few seconds before collapsing. I had no worries from bears or spoiled meat so took my time butchering. With the short days that time of year though, it was dark by the time I had gutted and skinned the animal, so I covered the carcass with a plastic tarp and snowshoed the approximately two miles back to my vehicle to return the next day. Glenn Elison returned with me, and a borrowed sled, to a very stiff moose carcass. If I had only taken a few more minutes to remove the quarters before abandoning the work the evening before our task then would have been much easier. Trying to move a solidly frozen whole moose carcass on a sled in deep snow was not fun. These are things you learn from, and try not to repeat. That bull was the farthest I ever had to transport; one caribou I packed nine miles; and several Dall sheep over the years were glued to my back for over 15 miles, but I exercised restraint on taking moose many times—the risk of losing all or some of the meat would frequently squelch my desire to fill my tag. In those cases, I suppose I shouldn't have been spending time in such faraway places anyway, if I was seriously moose hunting and not willing to undertake the backpacking if successful. I admit to often being struck by wanderlust in new country—just wanting to see what was over the next hill and then the next. Sometimes there would be a bull moose over that last hill, and there he would stay undisturbed, at least by me.

When we lived in Cold Bay, the kids were very young and still eating baby food. A small store and restaurant were available, but variety was little and prices high. Shannon and I ate one dinner at the Weathered Inn while living in Cold Bay and we paid $50 (1980s prices) for two hamburgers and milkshakes. Packaged food could be ordered, only in case lots, from Seattle and barged up several times a year. The whole community took part in such orders as few could use a case of ketchup or the like alone. We bought our baby food supply this way, but for some reason Gerber meats were not available. The kids got their protein from boiled and ground goose, caribou, or salmon which they seemed to relish, even without any seasoning.

It was not difficult to put up waterfowl, salmon, and berries while living in Cold Bay. Caribou were available too, but took a little more work. For variety, however, we sought out halibut whenever we might be able to catch one. Calm days were so rare in which one could safely launch a boat, when they did happen a lot of folks would take leave from work and go fishing. We also had the opportunity to use the city dock to fish from. Because it was designed to allow docking of the large Alaska State Ferry in a variety of tide conditions, the dock was built far out into the bay, allowing access to deeper water and the opportunity to catch halibut. The design did have some drawbacks however. The distance from the dock surface to the water was extreme—it was impossible to reel up a large fish to where it could be recovered. To retrieve a hooked halibut one had to gently reel it up just to the surface and then shoot it. Once dead, a grappling hook and rope were used to grab hold of the fish and winch it up onto the dock.

Fishing from the dock was therapeutic—the scenery across the bay was spectacular and the fishing good (halibut were relatively rare to bite but Irish lords/sculpin and cod were regular visitors to the bait, so it was never boring). Additionally, on occasion, I might catch a piece of history, like a chunk of Robert Jones' old Volkswagen (VW) Beetle. Bob "Sea Otter" Jones was a WWII veteran, spent nearly 30 years in the Aleutians, was the first manager at Izembek—spending weeks at a time working alone from a wood dory, and was a character. Rumor had it that Bob, when leaving Cold Bay, had stripped his vehicle of fuel, oil, battery, and such—rendering it clean and suitable for fish habitat, and pushed it off the dock. Few vehicles left Cold Bay. The wind ripped off doors, and the rain, volcanic dust, and salt air made short work out of any steel object. Bob was my supervisor when I worked in Savoonga, but had long retired when I moved to Cold Bay, so

I never got to ask him about the VW bug. Still, each time I hooked a rusty piece of something, I remembered Bob and smiled.

One evening I was fishing at the end of the dock when I heard a series of gunshots behind me. Rick Schlichten, who at the time managed Pavlof Services with his wife Jan, had apparently caught a halibut. After loading up my gear I drove back to where Rick was fishing and asked him, "How big?"

"Big," was the reply, "But it got away." After a little more dialog I learned that Rick had caught a large halibut, reeled it to the surface, fired five shots with his .357 Magnum, and believed he had killed the fish, but it had flopped a bunch and broke off. I asked where, and he pointed generally out over the water and kept fishing. I rigged up my rod with a series of 6.0 Gamakatsu hooks and weights and cast out over the general area where the fish had broken free and sunk. Within seconds my gear struck something on the bottom and I pulled up feeling a large dead weight that was moving ever so slightly with the retrieval of my line. As luck would have it I had hooked the dead halibut and began carefully bringing it to the surface. Rick had already set down his rod and made ready the grappling hook and rope, a smile emerging on his face. We pulled the fish up with the aid of Rick's truck, then weighed it before cutting it up. It was over 180 pounds. My share of the fillets provided a tasty alternative to salmon for months to come. We liked halibut second only to king crab.

THE COURTS – BIG CHANGES TO BIG GAME GUIDING AND SUBSISTENCE

Results from two legal challenges significantly changed the way Alaska managed its fish and game. The first was what was known as the Owsichek decision and it was rendered by the Alaska Supreme Court in 1988. The second, the McDowell decision, was decided by the same body the following year. In both cases, the Court overturned longstanding State management practices finding primarily that they were in contravention of the Common Use Clause of the Alaska Constitution. In *Owsichek*, the ruling threw out exclusive use areas in the State previously held by individual big game hunting guides. In *McDowell*, the State was stripped of its ability to give preference to the take of fish and game to rural residents, at least based solely on their zip code.

Implications of *Owsichek* were slow to be realized, unless you were one of the commercial guides that no longer had a guaranteed livelihood. The exclusive use guiding area program was managed under a set of State rules and administered by a State-established board. It did prevent many potentially qualified Alaskans from making their living guiding hunters, unless they were fortunate enough to get the nod from the Board, something that took many years of apprentice work for some, and never came at all for others. By losing the opportunity to restrict the number of commercial hunting guides, however, the State lost an important conservation tool. Whereas the previous system rewarded conservation by a guide limiting harvest within their exclusive use area as an investment for future years, its loss created a free-for-all. Guided trophy hunts became more market-driven, and restraint was not rewarded. If you didn't take a trophy animal from an area, somebody else probably would—get it while you can became the new mantra. Increased license sales and hunting pressure (fueled by a more affluent and mobile hunting public), various restrictions to hunting on some federal and Native lands, disease outbreaks, and localized predation impacts, all occurred over the same period of time. All of these factors, and perhaps others, contributed to the gradual deterioration of big game hunting quality and opportunity in Alaska the past few decades, but I believe the effects from *Owsichek* are probably most to blame.

A more familiar case to students of Alaska's game management history is *McDowell* v. *State* for it spawned a sea of change to fish and wildlife regulatory oversight and led to a dual management system that continues today. Like their ruling against exclusive guide areas, the Court found that providing a preference for use of fish and wildlife to certain citizens of Alaska, based solely on where they lived, was unconstitutional. The Constitution did allow for prioritizing uses and limiting some users based on the prioritization, but was determined to be limited to factors such as need rather than where a person might live. The rural residency requirement for the subsistence priority was a provision of Title VIII of ANILCA, and the State had worked to implement those legal requirements in applying State hunting and fishing regulations after its passage. After *McDowell* that was no longer legally possible. High-level discussions occurred in Juneau and Washington, D.C. in search for a manageable fix. A constitutional amendment was deemed the best approach by legal scholars, and was seemingly supported by a majority of Alaskans, but the idea of changing the Alaska Constitution to meet the requirements of an unpopular federal law did not sit well with some and the Alaska legislature would not act upon the amendment proposal. On July 1, 1990, federal land managers assumed responsibility for managing subsistence hunting on federal lands in Alaska—about 60 percent of the State. The initial regulatory announcement also included fishing on non-navigable waters; assumption of regulating the subsistence fishing for salmon and other fish in major river systems came later after additional litigation (significantly influenced by the Ninth Circuit Court of Appeals ruling in *Alaska* v. *Babbitt*, stemming from *Katie John* v. *United States*). While I remember well that federal managers, such as myself, were often accused by the public and media of taking over the State's control of fish and wildlife, such accusations were misleading at best. The root of the problem came from our elected officials crafting Title VIII in the way they did. They did so with the best intent, and the subsistence provisions of ANILCA were designed to address expectations and promises left unfulfilled in the Statehood Act and ANCSA. Lawmakers worked with the State on designing a system that recognized priority use for fish and game for those most dependent upon the resource and having the fewest options, and did so without basing it on race. When the system was later found legally wanting under State constitutional requirements, workable options were few. The system was not going to fix itself; it was a political hot potato fueling a growing rural/urban divide that created a no-win situation for politicians, and left to such devices, the outcome was left totally to the mercy of the Courts. Each major federal action implemented to fill the void post *McDowell* was driven by legal challenges, court decisions, legal opinions, and then more legal challenges, court decisions, and legal opinions. Federal managers were caught up in the legal road race, but most often were not positioned in the driver's seat.

Initially, regulatory changes affecting the take of fish and wildlife on federal lands were relatively few. Many of the changes were challenged and all were given significant scrutiny legally, biologically, and culturally. Over time the changes were more pronounced and the influence of the State over federal subsistence decisions diminished. At one point I suggested the process had become somewhat of a dance, and everyone knew the steps. A new proposal would be made by a regional subsistence council, the Federal Subsistence Board would hold a public hearing, ADF&G would testify in opposition, and then the proposal would pass. A dual management system became embedded into conservation decisions made for much of Alaska's fish and wildlife resources. Both State and federal processes persisted and both published separate regulations. Animosity grew as well as confusion. It is questionable whether any lasting harm was done to any fish or wildlife population from the dual and sometimes dueling processes, but the inefficiencies and seemingly avoidable conflict were obvious to all. It cried for a legislative fix, and still does.

While Alaska's Common Use Clause in its Constitution was laudable (and had the benefit of studying 48 others before its creation), it was not without flaw. This was evident earlier in State history when the necessity to create limited entry fisheries was successfully argued. Clearly every Alaskan that wanted to profit from commercially fishing for salmon could not be allowed to do so. Either limits would be so restrictive that no one then could make a living from the practice, or the opportunities would be so broad that the resource would be devastated. The problem was resolved in 1972 with a constitutional amendment that authorized limited use fisheries. Perhaps someday a similar effort will restore State authority over managing subsistence uses and allow more control over the commercial big game guiding industry. Fish and wildlife conservation would likely be better served if it does.

ON THE TRAPLINE

Like hunting and fishing, the trapping of furbearers is deeply rooted in Alaska's history and rural lifestyle. With limited means to come up with cash in much of Alaska, it is only logical that industrious people would find ways to capture and make use of animals around them that could be used to support themselves. This was done through direct use of trapped animals, or their barter for other goods, long before an international fur market was tapped into. In many ways, the former system of use was more dependable and sustainable—it was based on local needs and not on the whims of fashion in some faraway land. Like hunting and fishing, I also had the urge to run a trapline when I first moved to Alaska. Like many young men I imagine, I held an unreasonable dream of living the life of a trapper in the wilds, believing that I had been born 100 years too late. I knew also, however, if I had been born a century earlier it is unlikely I would have lived to see my eleventh birthday. I suffered an acute appendicitis as a boy on a summer fishing trip to a remote lake, riding one of our family donkeys out of the backcountry and being rushed into surgery just in the nick of time. Technology, and a burro named Cactus, had helped save my life. The dream of living in earlier, simpler times was unrealistic and perhaps a bit foolish, but then again, dreams can be such things.

I had trapped muskrats growing up in Oregon and made a few extra dollars in doing so. I also trapped a few raccoons but after seeing what they sold for I decided it wasn't worth taking their life for so little compensation. In Alaska I trapped muskrats too, but also foxes, ermine, mink, and other species. Marten were my primary focus. They were easy to catch, easy to skin, and brought an average of $42 when I sold them in town at the end of the season—a buyer would come to Fairbanks each spring and stay in a local motel where trappers would come to sell their catch. If prices were down, some trappers would hold back and wait for the following year, gambling that the wait would pay off in the end. Sometimes it did and sometimes it didn't. Lynx prices were particularly volatile; marten seemed to stay pretty stable.

I used a variety of traps and sets but my go-to setup for marten was a number one long spring trap stapled to a pole leaning up against a spruce tree. Once caught, the marten would swing free and not get its fur damaged by sap on the tree, or worse, be chewed by mice or shrews ruining the hide. I would bait the set by nailing a cisco (whitefish) head just above the juncture of the leaning pole and tree and would also use a drop of lure rendered from marten musk glands. It worked surprising well and I would average about six marten a week on a trapline of 40 or so sets.

I honestly had mixed emotions about trapping even in the early years. I loved being in nature and enjoyed the mystery and surprise when checking my sets. I acted humanely as possible, given the trade, and thought little at the time about taking the animals' lives for their fur. Still, something haunted me at times. I might have a dream about forgetting where my traps were or not being able to get out and check them, resulting in waste of animals. The event that influenced my thoughts the most, however, happened on a cold afternoon as I was finishing checking one of my traplines. A wolverine had been walking my line before me and had trashed a number of my sets and stole some of my catch. I was still following its tracks in the snow to my second to last set and the daylight had faded to the point I needed my double-mantle Coleman lantern to see my way as I snowshoed slowly along. As I approached the set, I saw a large frozen creature dangling from chain. It could not be the wolverine I thought. I had caught wolverine before and they were notoriously strong. There is no way one could have been subdued with this particular set up, yet there it was. In fact though, my initial assumption was correct—it wasn't the wolverine that had been raiding my line. It was a great gray owl, frozen, its wings partially stretched out making it look bigger than it actually was. It was a fluke of course, the owl probably didn't even see the bait on the tree, but just landed at the wrong place and wrong time.

Regardless of my care, I had sometimes captured a non-target animal, most often a gray jay, but this was different. Honestly I had seen no more great gray owls in my career at that point than I had wolverines, and I had just killed one by accident. They were protected of course, but such accidental take was rarely prosecuted. That wasn't the point. My take-home message to myself was that I didn't have any business setting traps and walking away from them to leave their capturing ability to chance. Others could trap, and have my full support, but as a federal biologist, under the watchful eye of many who didn't necessarily like what I stood for, I should not risk the activity. I would continue to hunt, for I could make an informed decision each time I pulled the trigger or released an arrow, but my control over what my traps might catch had less certainty—I gave up trapping.

THE FUTURE OF HUNTING

As the years passed I hunted less as the need for meat declined in our lives. I never gave it up though. I still prefer to eat wild venison that I have taken myself over anything I can buy in a store. The activity has also created deep bonds and friendships that go beyond any normal relationship. Good friends like Rickey Davidson, a retired FAA employee, has shared in creating many fond memories, from hunting wild turkeys in Missouri to Cape buffalo in Mozambique; or David Mathieson, longtime family friend, in chasing javelina in Arizona or kudu in South Africa; or Jim and Holly Akenson, former classmates at Eastern Oregon State and longtime wilderness managers of the Taylor Ranch in Idaho—sharing in pursuit of mule deer in Idaho to red deer in New Zealand; or Hanley Jenkins, Philip Commins, and Dale Borum, fishing for king salmon in Alaska or chasing elk in Oregon, and so many more. Sharing a hunting passion with like-minded companions in unique, and peaceful settings over extended periods of time, and with unpredictable results, cannot be easily replicated or ever forgotten.

It seems that much of society is supportive, or at least apathetical, about hunting when it is done for food. When done as recreation, with no real need for food, that support drops significantly. In truth, the line between sport and subsistence hunting can often be blurred. Few absolutely need to take wildlife to physically survive in this day and age, although exceptions are still evident in some of rural Alaska and in other subsistence-based regions around the world. The urge to hunt is primordial; it has a spiritual connection for many, it can provide healthy outdoor family activity, it allows people to connect with nature, and it can provide a healthier diet over food raised with hormones or grown with the aid of fertilizers and pesticides. Properly managed hunting can benefit wildlife populations even where the hunter is not the primary benefactor of the food they take. American hunters on safari in Africa cannot legally take meat home from any animal taken, yet none of it goes to waste. Even the entrails are generally used by local people, and all of the harvest is greatly appreciated. More importantly, the revenue brought in from foreign hunters gives the local wildlife economic value and promotes conservation. A great example is the hunting of lions. Though over-hunting can cause population concerns, properly managed hunting ensures the species' future. Lions are sustained because of the value to local communities from the hunting industry. In its absence, one concerned rancher might poison a whole pride in one night because of potential harm to their children or cattle; lions are viewed as competitors and a threat, much like wolves and grizzly bears were in the Lower 48 in the late 19th and early 20th century. Few practical alternatives exist also in managing populations of other wildlife in Africa, from springbok to elephants. Through no fault of their own, their historic habitats have been lost and the natural migrations over expanses of land have been lost too. Now, without some solution, such as regulated culling, some populations destroy their own habitat through over-grazing, condemning themselves and their kind to death through starvation. In some cases, the restoration of predators can help manage animal numbers, but in others, such as for elephants, the only effective predator is man. Poaching is always bad, but counterintuitive as it may seem, regulated hunting has a significant role to play in the conservation and ultimate preservation of many species throughout the world.

Hunting as an activity is diminishing in the world today. Practically I understand this—there are fewer hunting opportunities over time and the areas open to hunting are generally shrinking in size, more options for food are available in most places, and far more activities are also available to compete for free time. Philosophically, however, I do not understand the decline in hunting. If one holds that people are a mere artifact of evolution, the survival of the fittest permits the take of one animal for use by another, only limited by its own self-interest. This fits well with sustainable use conservation principles. If, however, one holds that people are beings created in the image of God, and given certain dominion over other lesser created creatures, responsible take of those creatures is also permissible. This too fits well with a conservation ethic and demonstrates respect for the supernatural Creator by respecting His creation and using it in an unselfish and sustainable manner. A philosophical debate nonetheless exists in the world today about the morality of hunting, and its future is uncertain. Should hunting continue to diminish as an activity, I know that Alaska, by law, necessity, and choice, will be one of the last places to restrict take of wildlife for human use. I know too that a hunter's heart, once formed, beats passionately until the hunter breathes their last.

Alaska law requires packing out all edible meat first – antlers are last.

Shannon and me with a 72-pound Kenai king salmon.

Bob "Sea Otter" Jones (about 1949).

On the trapline.

Chapter Ten:

THE MOOSE RANGE

While I was seeing old moose tracks and droppings at most places that I pulled the canoe ashore, the animals themselves were scarce. It wasn't until late in the evening on the fifth day of the trip that I spied the first moose, partially obscured in dense willows. He looked up briefly as I paddled by, having no apparent concern in my presence.

Most first-time visitors to Alaska, when asked what they hope to see, will list "a moose" fairly high on their wish list, along with a bear, a glacier, and Mt. McKinley. Alaska and moose seem to go together in peoples' minds like Egypt and pyramids or France and the Eiffel Tower. Unfortunately many visitors go home without seeing a moose, for in fact, there aren't that many of them given the size of Alaska, and frequently they are in places that can be difficult to visit. Alaska overall is more of a biological desert than a wildlife mecca. True, there are unique and wonderful animals to see there, but the living is tough and overall biological diversity and abundance are low.

A good place to generally see moose in Alaska is on the Kenai Peninsula, and I was fortunate enough to live and work there for 14 years as the Refuge Manager of the Kenai National Wildlife Refuge.

***

The Kenai Peninsula was known for its giant moose long before a road was built to there from Anchorage. Early visitors were attracted to the area first primarily in search of gold, to catch and can salmon, or trap and farm foxes for fur. Word of the area's giant moose attracted sportsmen, as early as 1897, who wrote about their exploits, which attracted more sportsmen. By the late 1920s the hunting opportunities were well known and well-advertised. A 1926 letter to "ALL CORRESPONDENTS" from the Alaska Glacier Tours Association, stated in part, "One of our guides, recently returned from our camp on the Kenai Peninsula, reports having counted over 1000 moose in one band. Specimens with a spread up to 80 inches have been shot on Kenai and you have a good a chance as anyone else to secure one of these record trophies if you hunt with us."

While the advertisement may have contained a bit of hyperbole, the hunting was good and the moose were large. The genetic makeup of Kenai moose, though not yet understood, did seem to result in larger moose than were generally known elsewhere, but also the population was responding to several factors that made them not only big but also abundant. The area was sparsely populated by people and developed roads, leaving large areas virtually undisturbed. Moose numbers were benefitting from a series of large fires (creating an abundant food supply as the burned areas regrew with young hardwood saplings). This happened at a time where the area also experienced a series of mild winters. Equally important perhaps, the few settlers living on the Kenai Peninsula had waged a war of sorts on predators. Bears and wolves were rare, the latter soon to be extirpated (though they returned on their own in later years). Under these conditions moose prospered and the hunting was excellent for those who paid the price of a steamship to Seward, had a month or so to spend in travel and pursuit of game, and a willingness to travel and live in a rough and unpredictable environment. This added all the more to the appeal to some of the early visitors seeking big game in Alaska. Travel to Kodiak in pursuit of giant brown bears grew in popularity at about the same time. Soon though, the reports coming back from Alaska were changing. Fears over poaching and overharvesting sparked advocacy for regulations and game refuges. Caribou had been eliminated from the Kenai Peninsula. Would moose be next?

Residents of the area generally favored the creation of a moose reservation, evidenced by a favorable editorial in the "Seward Gateway" in 1931, and citizens of Ninilchik petitioning for a moose preserve in 1932. Residents of Kenai seemed to be divided on the idea, with one major argument in opposition being that there were already too many laws not being enforced. The support for a specific land withdrawal for moose on the Kenai Peninsula still continued to grow, but each proposal would then generate a list of proposed exceptions by various interests, enough so the bureaucracy back in D.C. probably chose to let the kinks work themselves out before taking action. The moose protection ideas eventually fell to the FWS to develop further—FWS had been formed out of President Roosevelt's Reorganization Act of 1939 that initially transferred the Bureau of Biological Survey from the Department of Agriculture to the Department of Interior, and then combined them with the Bureau of Fisheries the following year. A copy of an old memorandum from the President sheds some light on a little of what he was trying to accomplish in Alaska, albeit with a little tongue and cheek. It read:

THE WHITE HOUSE

WASHINGTON

July 28, 1939

MEMORANDUM FOR

THE DIRECTOR OF THE BUDGET

I Agree with the Secretary of the Interior. Please have it carried out so that fur-bearing animals remain in the Department of Interior.

You might find out if any Alaska bears are still supervised by (a) War Department (b) Department of Agriculture (c) Department of Commerce. They have all had jurisdiction over Alaska bears in the past and many embarrassing situations have been created by the mating of a bear belonging to one Department with another bear belonging to another Department.

F.D.R.

P.S. I don't think the Navy is involved but it may be. Check on the Coast Guard. You never can tell!

Two pending land withdrawals at the time conflicted with the FWS-proposed moose refuge—one was from the army proposing the area as a training area and bombing range; the second was a proposal establishing an area to resettle potentially large numbers of Europeans seeking refuge from Nazi Germany. The refugee settlement proposal died in Congress and the FWS Director (Ira Gabrielson) convinced the army to choose an alternative location for bombing practice. On December 16, 1941, mere days after the bombing of Pearl Harbor, President Roosevelt signed Executive Order 8979, creating the Kenai National Moose Range (known widely as just "the Moose Range"). Even though ANILCA changed the name in 1980 to the Kenai National Wildlife Refuge, old-timers continued to refer to the Refuge as "the Moose Range" and do to this day. The purpose of the Moose Range was given as, "…protecting the natural breeding and feeding range of the giant Kenai moose on the Kenai Peninsula, Alaska, which in this area presents a unique wildlife feature and an unusual opportunity for the study, in its natural environment, of practical management of a big-game species that has considerable local economic value…"

The Kenai Peninsula would experience significant changes in the years following the establishment of the Moose Range. A road would be built connecting Anchorage to the Peninsula; oil would be discovered, resulting in leasing and eventually two operational oil and gas fields within the Moose Range; statehood resulted in transfer of property for municipalities and transportation needs; and ANCSA resulted in further withdrawals from the Moose Range to satisfy Native land selections. When ANILCA was being drafted, preexisting refuges like the Moose Range were given consideration for conservation needs, along with the proposed new refuges. Designating conservation areas and management objectives from the remaining federal estate (following the allocation of lands for the new state and to settle Native claims) would happen only once. There was some effort then to make the Moose Range whole again. The name was changed, boundaries were adjusted, nearly a quarter million acres were added, and Wilderness was designated on 1.3 million of the 1.9 million total acres. The purposes were changed too (paraphrased): to conserve all fish and wildlife and habitats in their natural diversity; fulfill international treaty obligations; ensure water quality and quantity; provide opportunities for research, interpretation, environmental education, and land management training; and to provide compatible opportunities for fish and wildlife-oriented recreation. Like ANILCA as a whole, changes to the Moose Range were met with both applause and disdain. One local group burned the refuge manager (Jim Frates at the time) in effigy when ANILCA was signed.

When I arrived at Kenai in the mid-1990s, the fervor over ANILCA had largely died down, but the Refuge was still viewed negatively by far too many people. I guess it can be the same in many places—government is to be distrusted and questioned. I felt my primary charge as refuge manager was to become part of the community, inform the public widely what rules and processes were in place and why, offer maximum flexibility for public involvement within those rules, and if consistent with the overall conservation mission of the Refuge, to amend the rules to meet public interests where possible. The Refuge was in the heart of the Kenai Peninsula and hundreds of people relied on it directly, and thousands indirectly, for their livelihoods. Whether someone made their living working in the oilfields or as a fishing guide, most did share common values when it came to quality of life—they supported clean air and water and abundant fish and wildlife. This shared connection to the land made my job easier.

Within a few years it seemed to me that the Refuge was better accepted in the local communities. I joined the Chambers of Commerce in Kenai and Soldotna, served on the Kenai Peninsula College Council, as a Board Member of the Kenai Convention and Visitor Bureau, and with the Kenai River Special Management Area Advisory Board. The Refuge held open houses, published a weekly article in the local newspaper, and expanded trails and built new recreational cabins. People only protect what they love and they only love what they can experience. The Refuge had to meet its primary wildlife conservation purposes, but it had to be available for people too. After all, the American people are its owners; refuge staff are just its caretakers. The staff was excellent. We had many talented biologists, maintenance workers, law enforcement officers, public use specialists, fire managers, and administrative staff. They made a good team, served the public well, and looked out for the critters. Challenges were frequent however. When managing nearly 2 million acres of land that had legal mandates ranging from resource extraction to wilderness protection, and with over 1 million visitors each year, stuff happens. Having a diverse and talented staff and a supportive community made the difference when challenges arose. It undoubtedly is the reason why I stayed in the position for 14 years. The job was both challenging and rewarding, and the community was a great place to raise our three children.

BLACK GOLD

While prospecting for gold at the end of the 19th century accounted for much of the early settlement of the Kenai Peninsula, those involved with the search for and development of oil resources easily surpassed those numbers in the mid-20th century. Some Alaskan historians believe that the discovery of oil near the Swanson River in the mid-1950s may have swayed Congress favorably in deciding statehood. What fears some might have had that Alaska would constantly need federal financial support based on its limited economy from salmon and some mining, were allayed considerably when "black gold" was added to the mix. The Nation was gaining an appetite for oil and Alaska had some.

Development of what was then still the Moose Range came under different rules than exist today. FWS had oversight of land management decisions, but the BLM oversaw minerals leasing programs, and the Secretary of Interior approved or denied resource extraction proposals based on advice from governors and other cabinet members and political realities. There was no guidance or restraint given from such future laws as the National Wildlife Refuge System Administration Act, National Environmental Policy Act, and the Administrative Procedures Act. The history of the discovery and production of oil on the Kenai is lengthy and at times a bit shady. Deals were cut, partnerships formed, and lobbying undertaken at the highest levels. Richfield Oil Corporation needed a coalition of Alaskan businessmen to apply for enough leases on the Moose Range to make the undertaking more viable; they were limited on what they could apply for themselves. Prominent businessmen also carried more weight when lobbying than did the oil company itself. With the stakes high, rival interests raised ethics questions about who would profit from oil lease decisions. A growing scandal threatened to land on the Secretary of Interior's doorstep and potentially remove him from office. Some BLM officials in Alaska did lose their jobs, but in the end, the July 1957 discovery on the Swanson River blossomed into an operational oil and gas field and the mystique of it origin faded. It would be joined by the development of another field, in the Beaver Creek area of the Moose Range, approximately 10 years later.

Along with multiple federal leases within the two operational oil and gas fields on the Refuge, Cook Inlet Region (an ANCSA-created regional Native Corporation) was granted entitlement to more than 200,000 subsurface acres of the Refuge and undertook exploration activities beginning in the 1980s. When I became the Kenai National Wildlife Refuge Manager, it was soon obvious that oil and gas exploration activities were legally embedded within a large portion of the Refuge, but were also prohibited from an even a larger portion: the 1.3 million acres Congress had set aside as Wilderness. What was uncertain was how the remaining 472,630 acres of Refuge, not bound by previous legal actions, were to be managed. Could they be leased too? Oil and gas development in Alaska drove most major economic and political discussions. At the forefront of many of these discussions for a number of years then was the State's desire to see the Coastal Plain (ANILCA 1002 area) of the Arctic National Wildlife Refuge opened to oil and gas exploration and development. Predictably, people looked to Kenai when developing their arguments, it being a refuge in Alaska that had operational oil and gas production underway for many years. What was difficult to process, however, was how people would use the information from Kenai. I would take one group on a tour of the oilfields and they would report how horrible it was for wildlife and habitat. I would take another group on the exact same tour and they would herald how great the oil and gas industry was getting along in helping the Refuge meet its conservation objectives. Kenai was being used as a tool to try to protect the Arctic Refuge on one hand and to try to open it on the other. The issue was largely apples and oranges to me. The Arctic had different species and different habitats. What worked one place, or was a problem, may or not apply elsewhere. What I could do, however, is summarize what we knew about oil and gas activities at Kenai. This I did in 1999 when I signed a compatibility determination that found oil and gas exploration and development activities were not compatible with the legal mandates for the Refuge established by ANILCA. We had years of data and ample evidence to conclude that overall the oil and gas activities on the Refuge had not contributed to Refuge purposes or been neutral. Measurable and often significant impacts to wildlife and habitats occurred and were likely to continue. Habitat alteration and loss, chronic contaminant problems, and disturbance to wildlife and Refuge users interfered with the purposes of the Refuge. The compatibility determination applied only to Kenai and only to the less than 500,000 acres of land that could still potentially be leased under the provisions of the Minerals Leasing Act. It could also be revisited if new information became available. Of course the finding was supported by some and not by others. It really shouldn't have shocked anyone. FWS is not a multiple-use agency. Congress can give new and specific direction at any time, but in the absence of that, FWS is charged in doing what is best for fish and wildlife for the continuing benefit of the American people.

Discussions of the fate of the Arctic National Wildlife Refuge continued. I remember speaking to the Council of Environmental Quality Chairman under President Bush about Arctic oil when he shared that maybe keeping the oil in the ground on the Refuge might best serve U.S. interests overall. By having a potentially large untapped petroleum reserve of our own, it might provide a better bargaining position for our nation in import negotiations with foreign oil producers. Hmm, I thought. Maybe, maybe not, but interesting. I often wondered how opinions of one or two people could sway a controversial decision. I have wondered too if the recent decision by Congress to provide for leasing in the Arctic 1002 Area wasn't as much to gather Senator Murkowski's support for the tax bill (after failing to do so on proposed health-care legislation) over any real perceived economic value. Perhaps, perhaps not, or perhaps some of both. The high-stakes politics of energy development often seem to fall second only to those of foreign wars and civil defense. I remember too Senator Stevens' position on the 1002 Area when asked why he was opposed to the development of the Pebble Mine in the Bristol Bay region but supported opening the Arctic Refuge to oil and gas development. His response was something like, "America needs oil. We don't need gold." And while America did need oil, Alaska really needed to develop is petroleum resources to pay its bills; it still does. It won't always be able to do so, but that is its current reality. What resources to develop, when, where, and how will always create conflict. It is politicians' job to decide how best to represent her or his constituents on such issues; it's a resource managers job to provide her or his best professional judgement and advice on such matters; and it is every American's right to speak up and try to influence the decision-making process. It's messy, but I don't know of a better way.

RUSSIAN RIVER

Even people who have never visited Alaska are often familiar with the annual scenes at the confluence of the Kenai and Russian Rivers. This is the site of the shoulder-to-shoulder "combat fishing" that occurs every summer in pursuit of sockeye salmon. It is the single most popular fishery in Alaska and it occurs on Kenai National Wildlife Refuge and Chugach National Forest—the Russian River forming the boundary between the two federal land units. The fishery has been important to people for thousands of years, evidenced by significant Dena'ina Athabascan and Kachemak tradition (Eskimo) archeological discoveries in the confluence area. The public risked losing this fishery twice in modern history. The first was from a natural event; the second from indirect actions made in an earlier attempt to open the Arctic National Wildlife Refuge to oil and gas development.

Over six decades ago, a naturally forming diversion in the headwaters of the Russian River threatened the clear water system. Skilak Glacier run-off was about to flow into Upper Russian Lake rather than the Resurrection River, filling the system periodically with silt and changing the system's productivity and sockeye fishery forever. The first Kenai refuge manager (Dave Spencer) jumped to action, along with help from others, walking an Army surplus D-7 cat over miles of rough terrain to build an earthen dam and prevent the diversion. Dave was soft-spoken and a kind family man but not afraid of a fight. He was dedicated to conservation, a strategic thinker, and a man of action. He enlisted in the navy shortly after the bombing of Pearl Harbor and became a pilot and flight instructor. His aviation skills were complemented by a strong aptitude for wildlife management enhanced by tutelage under Aldo Leopold. After the war he became a Flyway Pilot Biologist in Everglades National Wildlife Refuge (to become Everglades National Park) and left that positon in 1948 to come to Kenai. He soon became the refuge supervisor for all of the pre-statehood refuges in Alaska and was instrumental in establishing new protected areas as well as setting up survey and management programs. I had the pleasure of helping rename the Canoe Lakes Unit of Kenai Wilderness after Dave in 1997. It was only fitting to honor his legacy there as Dave had initially laid out and established the canoe routes through the Swan Lake and Swanson River systems that are now enjoyed by people from around the world. Dave passed away in

2000 at the age of 84, but his memory lives on. You can see the sign entering the Kenai Canoe System indicating the boundary of the Dave Spencer Wilderness. If you are willing to take a long hike, and know where to look, you can also still see an aged broken-down cat and an earthen dam in the headwaters of the Russian River.

The second time the public risked losing the Russian River fishery was due to a potential change in land ownership that could eliminate public access. Early in the Reagan Administration the first attempt was made to open the Arctic 1002 area to oil and gas development. Though Congress had put the issue aside for study and a future decision, the Secretary of Interior was seeking to use authority, granted by ANILCA, to trade lands under his management authority for other lands of equal value. The authority gave deference to the Secretary to adjust boundaries and conduct exchanges without bothering Congress for approval. The authority was to be used to enact what became known as "the mega trade"—subsurface acreage in the Arctic Refuge would be traded for equal valued Native lands within Interior managed conservation system units. A call went out to search for and build up "trading stock" and Section 14(h)(1) of ANCSA was the instrument of choice. The provision allowed the Secretary to withdraw and convey to appropriate Regional Corporations significant acreage of existing cemetery sites and historic places. Regional corporations would select lands, the Bureau of Indian Affairs would certify sites, and the BLM would adjudicate claims and convey title when appropriate. The mouth of Russian River was a logical site for selection. No one contested that the confluence area was the location of historical Native occupation, including cemetery sites, and Cook Inlet Region, Inc. (CIRI) made a series of selections.

The mega trade fell through. The discretionary use of the Secretary's exchange authority raised some eyebrows and, more importantly, the State of Alaska was objecting. The deal had been formulated without appropriate discussions with the State and at issue was not only the process but also a very large economic issue yet to be settled. The amount of royalties paid to the State from federal leases was a hot topic. Years later, however, the BLM was still stuck with certified 14(h)(1) sites that had not been conveyed. The circumstances behind the selections clouded the issue, but didn't change the legal reality and something had to give. CIRI could have reasonably forced the case in the courts, and may have turned a tidy profit for shareholders if the Russian River area was ultimately conveyed to them fee title, and then in turn developed into a high end exclusive fishing lodge or something similar. They entered negotiations in good faith however. They were truly interested in protecting the area's cultural resources, and representing their shareholders' interests, but not necessarily at the cost of taking the State's most popular sport fishery away from the public. Several years of negotiations took place between CIRI, the Forest Service, and the Kenai Refuge. In the end, legislation was drafted and enacted to ratify the agreement (PL#107-362 signed 12/19/02). All cultural artifacts would be transferred from the federal government to approved curation, some land would be transferred and easements granted, funding would be provided for construction of facilities, and the confluence area would remain in federal ownership and continued public access assured.

Today, the Russian River is still much as it has been for thousands of years: running full of crystal clear water, teaming with salmon, and available for the public to enjoy.

TALE OF TWO TUSTUMENA DECISIONS

Tustumena Lake is the largest lake on the Kenai Peninsula, and at approximately 73,000 acres, a significant feature of the Kenai National Wildlife Refuge. It lays at the base of benchlands—a Wilderness area inhabited by moose, caribou, bear, wolf, and wolverine. It is fed by glaciers, springs, and snow runoff; it drains into the Kasilof River and then into Cook Inlet and is home to salmon, steelhead, and lake trout. It is lined with historical cabins around its shore, and has an integral place in the area's history. It also is where the State of Alaska wanted to explore for oil in the 1960's, using derricks similar to those deployed in Cook Inlet.

While the federal government is often accused of abusing its power, it has been my experience that it generally restrains exercising the full authority granted under the Constitution. There is no doubt that a significant debate occurred among our nation's founders about the role of the federal government and the states from the onset. The Federalist Papers were crafted by Alexander Hamilton, James Madison, and John Jay in support of the proposed new Constitution defending the idea of a strong national government. Hamilton, early in his first thesis, wrote, "Among the most formidable of the obstacles which the new Constitution will have to encounter may readily be distinguished the obvious interest of a certain class of men in every State to resist all changes which may hazard a diminution of power..." Anti-Federalist Papers, penned by such statesmen as Patrick Henry and John DeWitt published dissenting opinions. Henry wrote on June 7, 1788, "This Constitution is said to have beautiful features; but when I come to examine these features, Sir, they appear horridly frightful: Among other deformities, it has an awful squinting; it squints towards monarchy: And does not this raise indignation in the breast of every American: Your President may easily become King: Your Senate is so imperfectly constructed that your dearest rights may be sacrificed by what may be a small minority; and very small minority may continue forever unchangeably this Government, although horridly defective: Where are your checks in this Government?"

Though the federalists eventually won the debate and the Constitution was ratified by the States, the arguments largely remained unchanged over time, including among those in power in the new State of Alaska. The strong national government was ceded power from the original 13 colonies/states, to go on to grant conditional sovereignty to all new states, reserving some power, but tempering it with anti-federalism policies and orders. Some administrations have shown more deference and restraint in dealing with the states over others, but all seem to draw the line on significant issues of jurisdiction and economics. The Tustumena Lake case entailed both issues.

The new State of Alaska claimed the bed of Tustumena Lake, and any wealth in resources it might hold. Additionally, the subsurface estate was deemed dominant. The State held that access for oil and gas exploration could not be denied by the Refuge. Unlike future jurisdictional disagreements that were allowed to exist unchallenged in court (like FWS and the State both laying claim to Skilak Lake—the former as part of an existing Refuge and the later as part of a State Park), the Tustumena drilling proposal could not be left without challenge. In time, the Ninth Circuit Court of Appeals (1970) would hold that the Executive Order withdrawing the Kenai National Moose Range appropriated lands and waters delineated with specific metes and bounds and for specific purposes and that none of those lands and waters passed to the State upon statehood. The Supreme Court denied certiorari and the decision stood. Future challenges decided by the Supreme Court (Dinkum Sands/Arctic National Wildlife Refuge, 1997, and Glacier Bay, 2005) were resolved similarly: pre-statehood reservations of land and water did not pass to the State under the equal footings doctrine or Submerged Lands Act. One cannot really blame the State of Alaska for the position they took in these cases. If they sued for quiet title on any claimed property interest, it might not be challenged—What did they have to lose? The federal government is a big boy. It can always decide whether the stakes are high enough to defend its interests, or whether to sit tight and bite its lip.

The second Tustumena decision addressed salmon enhancement activities. When I first became the Kenai Manager I was asked to permit Tustumena salmon enhancement as an established operational activity, regulated by the State—it had been permitted conditionally as a research activity previously. ADF&G had initiated the work years before but had contracted it to the private non-profit Cook Inlet Aquaculture Association (CIAA) in 1993. Both ADF&G and CIAA sought assurances that the activity would be allowed to continue. The project entailed a temporary camp at the mouth of Bear Creek on Tustumena Lake. A weir was placed in the creek each summer and approximately 10,000 sockeye salmon were captured to yield about 10 million eggs. The eggs would be taken off the Refuge (to Trail

Lakes Hatchery) to incubate and the fry (approximately 6 million fish) would be returned to the mouth of Bear Creek and released the following year. The practice greatly increased survival and enhanced the natural sockeye run substantially. This benefited wildlife and sport and personal use fishermen, but was primarily of benefit to commercial fishing interests in Cook Inlet. Opposition came from sport fishing groups. An enhanced salmon run meant longer fishing times for sockeye by set-netters which resulted in increased non-target catch of king salmon—prized by sports fishermen. Tustumena Lake was also in Wilderness designated by ANILCA and Wilderness advocates opposed permitting projects that altered natural processes; such things were generally prohibited by law.

I delayed the permitting request with CIAA until they could complete an environmental analysis—something necessary to transition from a research project to an operational one. The project also had enough environmental concerns and associated controversy that I requested an Environmental Impact Statement (EIS) rather than an Environmental Assessment (EA). CIAA, the State, and Alaska's Congressional Representative pushed back—an EIS is much more time-consuming and expensive than an EA. They didn't support doing either, but the EIS was a non-starter. It looked like we were at a stalemate and the operation might proceed without a permit, calling the Refuge's hand. I gave a little and offered that a mitigated EA could be completed. This was a rarely used option that could result in a finding of no significant impact if (legally binding) mitigation measures were in place to address potential negative impacts. There was just enough time to still complete this process and the compromise was accepted. While the mitigated EA was being drafted, I asked for a second Solicitor's opinion—the first didn't fully satisfy me on the two core legal questions: (1) Was the proposed project inconsistent with the Wilderness Act's requirement to maintain natural conditions within the Wilderness? and (2) Did the proposed project constitute a commercial activity precluded by regulations? The second legal opinion expanded upon the early view—the activity could be legally permitted under the Wilderness Act and Refuge regulations. After the EA was completed, it was signed by the Regional Director, and I issued a Special Use Permit, including all the stipulations addressed in the EA. The Wilderness Society and the Alaska Center for the Environment quickly filed suit (1998).

The district court decided against the plaintiffs. Supplemental records were submitted in request for further review and the district court denied the plaintiffs' motion. Appeal was made to the Ninth Circuit. The district court decision was affirmed by panel and filed January 13, 2003.

I am not sure why the court took up the case again, but a strongly worded dissent on the panel's decision certainly had influence in rehearing en banc by the Ninth Circuit. On December 30, 2003, they reversed and remanded their earlier decision, concluding that the district court erred in finding the enhancement project not to be a commercial enterprise, something Congress had specifically prohibited in designated Wilderness. The Alaska Senate passed a resolution requesting Congress to amend the Wilderness Act to authorize fishery enhancement programs in Wilderness, but no changes followed.

Limits to what kind of management activities can occur in Wilderness are commonly held as reasons by some state managers opposed to Wilderness designations. Their objections are based on very real restrictions; however, without such protection, the inevitable erosion of America's wild areas would occur. Some will be diminished or lost anyway, but Wilderness protection slows the process overall. Today Tustumena Lake is largely as it was a century ago. There are no roads around its shore, no oil derricks in its waters, and historic salmon runs still make their annual appearance.

REFUGE COMPATIBILITY

When the Moose Range was first opened to oil and gas development no organic legislation existed for the National Wildlife Refuge System that guided its management. Big decisions were made by high-level bureaucrats; lesser decisions were made by field managers. All decisions were made by whatever seemed best, often with only generic legislated guidelines. In 1966, Congress passed the National Wildlife Refuge System Administration Act. Its origin came from concerns that refuge management decisions were not always benefiting fish and wildlife like they should and that FWS had been too frequently passing management responsibilities onto other entities, particularly the states. The 1966 Act required that all uses of refuges must be found to be compatible with their established legal purposes and that only FWS could have oversight over refuge management. Significant amendments came to the Act in 1997; the amended law is commonly referred to as the Refuge Improvement Act, or simply "the Improvement Act."

The original push behind the Improvement Act came from a desire by some members of Congress to make hunting a purpose of the National Wildlife Refuge System. Such a designation could ensure hunting was viewed as a compatible activity on refuges and counter what was believed to be an erosion of refuge hunting programs and their overall support. A Republican majority in Congress voiced a growing support for such action, but Secretary Babbitt (Clinton Administration) and high-level Department and FWS officials, like Dan Ashe, worked with Congressional members to enhance refuge protection while increasing focus on hunting and fishing and other wildlife-dependent recreational activities. It made little sense for hunting to be a purpose throughout the entire System, such as for a tiny refuge established specifically for an endangered species, but it also was clear that a hunting heritage was part of Refuge System history—millions of acres within the System had been added because of hunters' support and financial contributions—and opportunities certainly existed to enhance hunting opportunities around the Country. Compromise language in the final bill made hunting, fishing, wildlife observation, wildlife photography, environmental education, and interpretation to be priority public uses on national wildlife refuges. Refuge managers were tasked to work with state fish and game agencies to develop and implement quality wildlife-dependent recreation programs when compatible with the legal purposes for which individual refuges had been established.

Congress gave FWS two years to complete regulations to implement the Refuge Improvement Act changes to determine compatible uses. In essence, this was the legal framework for refuge managers everywhere to determine what may or may not be allowed on the land they were charged with managing. I could think of no single greater task facing the National Wildlife Refuge System for the foreseeable future and volunteered to help with the process. With input from all FWS regions, able management of Jim Kurth, Ken Edwards, and others in the Washington Office, and public involvement in all draft policies and rulemaking, we completed the implementing rules and polices and then created training materials and delivered a two-day course to managers across the Country. Two of the contributions to the final product that I was most proud of included language specific to absolute criteria on what could be found compatible, and language specific to certain refuge lands in Alaska. These elements are found at 603 FW2.5A and 50 CFR 25.21(b)(1), respectively.

Final policy included in the FWS manual for refuge management informed that, "… Fragmentation of the National Wildlife Refuge System's wildlife habitats is a direct threat to the integrity of the National Wildlife Refuge System, both today and in the decades ahead. Uses that we reasonably may anticipate to reduce the quality or quantity or fragment habitats on national wildlife refuge will not be compatible." This hard line in the sand made it difficult to kill a refuge over time through "a thousand paper cuts"—Congress could always direct changes to address public interest, but FWS managers could not be pressured into uses that slowly eroded a refuge's ability to achieve its mandates. Other provisions in policy allowed for mitigating damages (such when considering to permit a new right-of-way) but any lost habitat or its value to wildlife had to be replaced before finding the use compatible.

The Alaska-specific provisions in the rulemaking addressed ANCSA 22(g) lands. When Congress was deciding the fate of Alaska Native claims settlement legislation, different versions of the bill were considered. Some proposals put off limits (for selection) any federal lands that had previously been set aside for specific purposes. The final version, however, removed some federal lands from selection (like military installations and national parks) and left others available (in this case pre-statehood national wildlife refuges) but required that any lands conveyed from existing refuges be subject to a first right of refusal if ever sold, and that the lands be subjected to the laws and regulations governing use and development of the refuge (ANCSA Section 22(g) "covenant"). This had become an awkward provision in ANCSA ever sense its passage in 1971. Refuge managers frequently viewed the language to mean 22(g) lands must be treated the same as the rest of the refuge, but this hardly made sense to Native landowners. Over the years neither side moved much on their positions and the issue became the proverbial can kicked down the road. The Refuge Improvement Act gave opportunity to resolve the stand-off in the congressionally mandated compatibility rulemaking. At issue was over one million acres on six Alaska refuges, including Kenai. The final rule clarified that a compatibility determination was required for uses of 22(g) land, but the process would differ significantly. It would have to be done only once (when a new use was proposed), and uses would be found not compatible only if they spilled over to negatively impact the "mother" refuge. The determination was not to consider potential damages to the 22(g) land itself, only refuge lands affected by the proposed use. In this way the integrity of refuges was protected yet Native landowners had near complete autonomy over use of their conveyed lands. Like most compromises, few were totally happy with the rule, but no one challenged it either. The issue was settled.

A CHANGING CLIMATE

Kenai National Wildlife Refuge celebrated its 75th anniversary in 2016. Because of its location and uses, it has generally been well staffed and has been able to do some incredible science. With this talent and time, the Refuge has become a centerpiece for studying changes: climate; fire regimes;

aquatic and terrestrial habitats; fish and wildlife numbers; invasive plants, animals, and diseases; and human uses. When the Refuge's Comprehensive Conservation Plan was completed in 2010 it reflected back and documented many observed changes. Mean annual temperature had warmed several degrees since the late 1970s and available water decreased significantly. Tree lines rose, ponds dried up, glaciers receded, and fire seasons lengthened. A spruce bark beetle outbreak, fueled by warmer temperatures, infested hundreds of thousands of Refuge acres. Managers began to grapple with how to adapt programs to address climate change. The task continues to be perplexing, but having long-term monitoring data for large areas is critical to making informed decisions. The issue of adaptation (for wildlife) was just beginning to warm up by itself when I left Kenai. I have followed many of the cutting-edge publications regularly produced by Refuge staff, active and retired, and am extremely proud. The world needs more folks like them. Collectively they will make a difference.

The climate changed for me too after 14 years at Kenai. We raised our family there. I had promised the kids that once they were in high school I would not transfer (on my own doing) until they had graduated. Towards the end of 2009 they were all in college in Anchorage. Alexandra (Alex) was studying to be an engineer, Remington (Rem) started in biology and then switched to process technology, and Hannah was on a fast track to be a teacher. Shannon left her position teaching science and math at Kenai Middle School, we sold the house, loaded our Welsh terrier and German wire-haired pointer into two heavily laden vehicles and headed south to Portland to help administer refuges in the Pacific Northwest and the Pacific Islands. Kenai had a lasting influence on all of us and hopefully we did some good for the Kenai too. It is a special place.

Kenai National Wildlife Refuge.

Some of Kenai Refuge's Managers (L to R) Dave Spencer and wife Eloise, John Hakala, Jim Frates, the author, Bob Seemel, and Will Troyer.

Sockeye salmon in Bear Creek – Tustumena Lake.

The Kenai Peninsula is a great place to raise a family
(Above – Hannah, Alex, and Rem).

Chapter Eleven:
KING FOR A DAY

The river environment had not seemed to change much in 40 years. At least it didn't feel different and really, why should it? The presence of the Park Service in the Upper Yukon was evident only if you visited the few cabins they maintained along the way, or in some of the boat traffic on the river supporting maintenance of the cabins, field studies, or patrols. I surmised that I could tell the difference between government employees and their boats versus the locals. Perhaps I was correct, but the passing of other vessels as I paddled downstream was almost always at some distance and without any verbal exchange—I didn't really know. I based my conjecture on the type of craft, description of the occupants, and what they were wearing—in one case everyone was donned in brightly colored floatation suits—almost certainly not locals headed to their fish camp. I gathered too that much of the animosity toward the Park Service had disappeared over time and their presence seemed welcomed by many, or at least held with ambivalence rather than disdain.

Having been a government employee in Alaska for 30 years, I got used to the variety of treatments, everything from anger and stares to jokes and compassion. Folks living in the more remote reaches rarely had much time for any government official. For non-Natives, their choice of living location was probably based as much on a general dislike for cities, structured social interactions, and official rules, as much as anything. Native villages varied greatly depending on how dependent on a subsistence lifestyle they were, how close they were to an urban center, their size, and other factors such as tribal leadership and whether they were dry or not. Dry villages allowed no alcohol use, whereas wet villages did (and "damp" villages allowed private use but no sale or distribution). Alcohol was often the root cause of serious crime in villages, as well as a significant factor in the long-term health and productivity of both individuals and communities.

Native Alaskan attitudes toward the government were generally respectful, questioning, and protective. Most elders had witnessed many government decisions over time that drastically affected their people and were sometimes disturbed if not bitter over some of them. I often thought much of the bitterness and mistrust came from basic cultural differences. When a government official first visited village elders to discuss some potential management action, two different views of the meeting seemed to take place. For the government official they often felt they were doing due diligence in public involvement by scoping out alternatives and describing potential outcomes. For the village leaders, they seemed to believe that if they spoke their wishes to the official, their recommendations would be enacted. Why else would someone travel to their community and seek the counsel of the elders?

Urbans dwellers generally fell into one of three groups. The first were tied to a conservative political base and leery of most all government. Many of these folks were politically active. They got involved with the planning and decision-making processes. Most, though never likely to support government controls, were value-added to the process. A few were not. They were conspiracy theorists and seemed often to lack basic logic. Occasionally I could switch gears in conversation and initiate meaningful give and take. My response to claims of government conspiracy usually would be, "Believe me, I have worked for the government for a long time—we couldn't pull off such a conspiracy if we wanted to", or "Would you mind giving me your social security number so I can cross reference it with our satellite data? It helps inform where to send our black helicopters." The first statement I actually believed; the second of course I did not, but it sometimes lightened the mood a little.

The second group were supporters—either with a conservation focus or just in support of good government in general. The third were apathetical, poorly informed, or both. They didn't vote, didn't know the difference between the Alaska Department of Fish and Game and the FWS, and probably didn't know or care who the governor was. This last group was the most challenging. Meaningful discussions could occur, even if there was disagreement, when there was at least one common value. For example, I remember many heated debates about resource allocation, primarily between commercial fishermen and sport fishing interests. At the end of the day, however, both groups prospered when the fisheries were healthy, and both were harmed when the fisheries were depleted. You have to have fish and wildlife in order to fight over fish and wildlife. The common ground over caring for the resource is a workable starting point for all resource-related disagreements. If there was disregard for the resource by one of the parties, it was very difficult to make any progress.

The river was devoid of almost all trash—I saw no bottles or cans floating downstream, and it was rare to see any type of garbage washed up on the banks either. It was even rare to see a human footprint when walking the beaches after pulling the canoe in for the evening. Other than a couple of presumed government craft, and two barges run aground in mid-river, the only human presence was people traveling back and forth from salmon fishing sites. The barges were loaded with large boulders and heavy equipment. I assumed they were headed for Fort Yukon and just ran out of water given their heavy loads—waiting for fall rains to float them again. I didn't really know. People accessing the fishing sites were frequently single men, but were just as often extended families. They fished with nets and fish wheels. The fish wheels were particularly intriguing to me. They needed to be placed perfectly—harnessing the river's power to turn the "scoops" but in a controlled fashion so as not to tear apart or wash away in the current—close to shore but far enough out, in just the right place, to intercept fish swimming upstream. The mechanical noise of the arm of the wheel turning slowly in the current echoed across channels and sloughs like a very slow grandfather clock. As I watched these devices at a distance I would wonder whether a particular turn of the arm would deliver a fish to the adjacent trough. I thought at times I could hear the flopping of a recently captured king salmon, but then the sound would disappear and only the creaking of the turning fish wheel and sudden noise of it completing its cycle would be heard, and then a few minutes later, I would be too far downstream to hear even that.

The migrating salmon on the Yukon River are a shared international resource. Some remain in Alaska, but others travel the over 1,200 miles to Canada and continue to spawning areas from there. Their harvest by commercial fishermen for the one to five years they are in the ocean is restricted, but once returned to freshwater, they can be taken by subsistence fishermen during their entire journey to their natal streams. They are an extremely important resource for the people living along the river. There are years of strong returns and others where the runs are so low that protective measures have to be employed to ensure adequate escapement for the future. In the years of low returns, communicating conservation needs to locals can be difficult; their ability to find adequate alternative resources for the year likely even more difficult. The federal government, because of ANILCA, court decisions, and the inability of Alaska to manage subsistence take of fish and wildlife based on rural residency, now finds itself charged with managing the Yukon River salmon fishery to ensure the conservation principles are followed while providing subsistence harvest opportunity. It ought not to be that way. Local people's needs should have a priority over commercial and sporting uses, but should never come at the expense of sustainability.

Canada should have a portion of the return allocated them as they provide a portion of the critical spawning habitat (and their Native people have no less a tradition of using salmon than those in Alaska). But the State of Alaska should be managing the program, consistent with the above management parameters, not the federal government. Even on the larger federal conservation system units, primary management of the fisheries and resident game should fall to the State, with as few as deviations as necessary from State rules to meet particular federal requirements. The animals don't know where the boundaries are—whether they are within areas of federal or State jurisdiction. If I were king for a day, I would fix that.

So why in the past 30 years has the issue of dual management not been resolved? The answer is simple: people are unwilling to compromise. I don't understand this. A constitutional amendment for Alaska would grant management responsibility for fish and wildlife for 100 percent of the State for perhaps 95 percent of the time. As things are, they have such responsibility for 40 percent of the State for 100 percent of the time. This is an oversimplification, but the premise is not that far off. Politically it is a red herring. People in rural areas support a rural preference; people who don't live in rural areas are as a rule not as fond of the arrangement. But the lines are fuzzy. Consider getting a telephone poll asking whether you believe that people who live in rural areas with few options for obtaining food ought to have preference in taking fish and wildlife over those who live in urban areas with more alternatives to obtain food. Most would probably respond favorably. But consider getting the same type polling question, only this time you are asked whether you believe that all Alaskans should be treated equally, and all should have equal access to the State's natural resources. Again, most would probably respond favorably, but the response is in direct conflict with the first question. There lies the conundrum. Alaska has demonstrated innovative ways to provide preference to rural residents, such as requiring antlers to be sawn in two (reducing trophy hunting) or only issuing permits in local villages well in advance of a hunt (thereby requiring non-locals to travel at least twice to participate in the particular opportunity), but these become legal games. How much better it would be to set seasons and bag limits and methods and means based first on conservation principles and second on what works best for all user groups, but yes, with priority given to customary and traditional take in rural Alaska. I believe this could best be addressed through an amendment to the Alaska constitution. Alaskans have been split on this, but have generally favored both a state-managed system and rural preference. A 1982 statewide ballot initiative to repeal the State subsistence law (that aligned with ANILCA requirements) failed with 59 percent of Alaskans voting in opposition. With federal takeover looming in 1990, in special session, the legislature failed to pass a constitutional amendment bill with a vote of 26 to 14 (a two-thirds majority was required to pass, needing 27 favorable votes). That bill would have prevented the federal takeover, given the ultimate decision to the people (in a vote four years later), and would have given time to pursue the only two other conceivable options: amend ANILCA or legally challenge ANILCA on constitutional grounds. Both of the alternatives were out of control of Alaskans; the constitutional amendment was not. It still is the best choice for resolution of this unique problem.

There is no one size fits all for subsistence and that is probably part of the reason some people throw darts at the rural preference provisions, because of some tough questions. What is rural? Will what was once rural always be rural? Do customary and traditional uses evolve (can a rifle be used in place of a harpoon)? ANILCA addressed these issues in a cursory manner, but the courts have provided most definition that affected implementation. This is one area that "friendly" amendments to ANILCA could clarify; however, not without risk. Any adjustments to definitions create winners and losers, and any opportunity to open ANILCA for discussion would likely become a political Christmas tree with every interest imaginable trying to hang an ornament on it.

The Kenai was not immune from the subsistence debate. Parts of the Kenai Peninsula were determined to be rural and other parts not. Such a situation disenfranchised Kenaitze Indian people if they lived in town, but allowed for a rural preference for any Alaska resident, regardless of race, if they lived in an area determined to be rural—no matter their income and no matter their length of residency (as long as they were residents—residing in the State for at least a year). It didn't take long for qualified rural residents to start seeking preference using the new federal process, first for moose, and later for fish. The Kenai Refuge was legally different that the other Alaska refuges. Its legal purposes, established by ANILCA, included a mandate to provide for fish and wildlife–oriented recreation. It did not have a purpose, as all other refuges, to provide the opportunity for continued subsistence uses by local residents. Being the odd unit out, left Kenai to be absorbed by processes established for the rest of "federal" Alaska, including not only refuges but also all national parks, BLM lands, and national forests. I maintained that Kenai must also provide for rural preference, consistent with Title VIII of ANILCA, but in doing so had to also ensure that the use was compatible with its specific legal purposes. I held that subsistence priority could impact recreational opportunity, but not to the point that a wildlife-oriented recreational use would be lost in order to provide for subsistence. During my tenure that threshold did not happen, but it could be on the horizon and may have to be decided by the courts. One area I held fast on was the use of gill nets on the Refuge. I believed that they had a legitimate use for subsistence and commercial uses, but that they were indiscriminate killers, entangling and killing unintended species such as loons and beavers, and also provided safety risks on a busy river where boaters could foul a prop unintentionally and lose power in swift current. As such, I believed that gill nets should not be used on the Kenai River within the Refuge. The use was not formally proposed before I left and no compatibility determination was completed. I noted, however, that subsistence gillnet use was permitted in the summer of 2016, following a bump in king salmon escapement and a threat of litigation. It seemed a slippery slope of politics, social issues, and biology.

Paddling a gentle stretch of water gave ample time for reflection, not only on the subsistence dilemma, but on government in general. What if I was king for a day? Not going to happen, but fun to consider; kind of like pondering what you would do if you won the lottery and had $100 million to spend.... My mental list grew fairly rapidly. First, I would get rid of the political party system. Conservation, and in fact all government programs, should not belong to a political party and I largely found that to be true, with some exceptions. During my tenure I worked under six presidential administrations, three Democrat and three Republican. Laws didn't automatically change when someone new took office and changes to policy direction were generally slow to come. In the earlier years too it seemed that an incoming administration would generally honor what was accomplished in previous ones, even if they didn't like it. There was an acceptance that change had come through a legitimate process and a focus was made on looking forward rather than back. One of the obvious differences between party platforms was the Arctic National Wildlife Refuge. All Republican administrations supported opening the refuge to oil and gas; all of the Democrat administrations favored its protection. For managers it was important to understand that such issues were a political pendulum—don't get too vested in the position of one administration so as to get hit when the pendulum swings back the other way. Of course there is nothing wrong with political parties taking stands on key issues, but no political system is faced with only one or two issues. Blind loyalty to a party has advanced to where it can blur common sense. Alexander Hamilton referred to parties as a "most fatal disease," and George Washington cautioned that an overly successful party would create "frightful despotism." America has allowed other parties to come into power for a time, such as the Whig Party, but has largely fallen to a two-party system. To me such lack of diversity hobbles our great nation. Basically a conservative, I was a registered Republican like my father and his father before him. In retirement however, disillusioned too often by party politics, I registered as "unaffiliated." I still vote of course, but I vote my conscious—not beholding to a particular party. Such a choice comes with a cost—I am unable to vote in the primary. I have no voice in selecting candidates until they are provided to me on a ballot in the general election. If I was king for a day, that would change.

Dreaming on, I thought of other changes I would make. I would do away with the tax code and transition to a flat tax: if you made a little, you would pay a little; if you made a lot, you pay a lot. Those below congressionally determined poverty level would be exempt but all other would pay a percentage of their earnings (without exemptions) based on rates set by Congress, and that could not be changed more often than every four years unless approved by a super majority vote. Wouldn't it be nice to file your income taxes on a post card? I would also institute term limits and meaningful campaign finance reform. A guy can dream right?

Overall I was pretty happy being a civil servant. I traveled enough to see how other countries ran their business and pretty much settled on the old United States being as about as good as it gets. The founders acknowledged that they didn't get everything perfect (forming a more perfect union, not a perfect one) but they also created processes for the people to make changes as changes were warranted. As I advanced from a field biologist to an administrator, I had only one recurring complaint. I really disliked being beat up by members of Congress for implementing laws that they had passed. The Executive Branch has a lot of power granted by the Constitution and even greater power when so authorized by the Congress, but it doesn't make the laws. The Judicial Branch has a lot of power, interpreting acts of Congress, settling disputes among people, corporations, and states, and deciding the fate of people, but they don't make the laws. Our elected representatives and senators have the power of the pen—they can make laws, amend laws, and repeal laws. They have the real power and that is the way the founders set up our government – checks and balances yes, but with the power reserved to the people through their elected officials. So when a representative or senator decided to threaten an agency in objection to implementation of federal law, I had to bite my lip. Sure, the Endangered Species Act or Clean Water Act or a whole host of other laws are unpopular in some circles, but that should never be taken out on those doing their job to implement them. If agencies are implementing laws in a manner unattended by Congress, Congress should amend and clarify. If courts interpret a law in a manner unintended by Congress, Congress should amend and clarify. I know that even if I was a king for a day, I couldn't fix that problem. Only Congress could.

Chapter Twelve:
TEETH AND CLAWS

The Tatonduk River is the first significant tributary flowing into the Yukon below Eagle, but it is easy to miss unless one carefully examines the distant terrain and has studied a topographic map. Such is true for all of the tributaries really, as the Yukon is flat and wide and the view sitting in a canoe is not very revealing of distant geographic features that are essentially at the same height as the paddler. I remember camping at the mouth of the Tatonduk River 40 years ago. It is where I caught my first Arctic grayling and where I saw my first wolf.

On this trip I didn't see a wolf or catch a grayling when I visited the confluence of the Tatonduk and Yukon. I did beach the canoe and walk upstream of the clear tributary a short distance, fishing rod in hand. I hadn't gone too far though when I noticed movement in the willows ahead. It was either a moose or a bear—large and brown. I studied the form moving slowly ahead of me and then saw the tell-tale hump over the large shoulders of a mature grizzly bear. He didn't know I was there and I thought best to keep it that way. I returned to the canoe and looked elsewhere for my dinner.

Wolves and bears in Alaska have been the heart of much debate over time. They compete with human interests, and on occasion can threaten human lives (though wolf attacks on humans are all but unheard of). I saw wolves on this trip too, as well as both black bears and grizzly. Their sightings enhance the wild experience, and I wouldn't wish it any other way. That said, bears deserve respect and I always camped where I could see well in all directions, kept a clean camp, and carried both a shotgun and bear spray.

In the early Alaska territorial days, bears, along with wolves, were treated as predators and furbearers, and their hides were traded and sold. A primary job of early federal agents in the territory was to control predators and they were trapped and poisoned. Bounties were paid, and around 1950, aerially shooting was also initiated to reduce predator populations and promote higher numbers of ungulates that were important for human food (primarily moose and caribou). Early after statehood in 1959, the new legislature outlawed poisoning of predators, and bounties were soon eliminated too. In 1963 wolves were reclassified by the Alaska Board of Game to be both a fur animal and a big game animal but aerially shooting was still allowed. The activity became popular among some of the public in the 1960s. The practice, by the public, was discontinued after the passage of the (federal) Airborne Hunting Act in 1972, but State management activities continued (by aerial gunning of wolves) in some areas where declines in prey populations were sought to be reversed. The management efforts proved to be highly controversial with the public in Alaska as well as nationally, and the program went through a series of fits and starts influenced by a variety of proposed laws and regulations and legal challenges. In the early 1990s a national effort, spearheaded by animal rights organizations, started a boycott campaign that threatened Alaska's tourism industry unless wolf control was halted.

After coming into office in 1994, Governor Tony Knowles suspended wolf control efforts and contracted for a review of the State's predator management programs by the National Research Council. Their work, entitled: *Wolves, Bears, and Their Prey in Alaska: Biological and Social Challenges in Wildlife Management*, took a year to complete and was published in 1997. The report concluded that some predator control efforts could be successful in increasing numbers of prey species but that such programs should always be scientifically based (sound science must indicate the likelihood of success), economically prudent (programs shouldn't spend tens of thousands of dollars to "make" only a handful of more moose), and socially acceptable (the public overall must be accepting of how "their" resource is being managed for public benefits). Hoping to provide some direction consistent with State constitutional objectives and steer State managers through the unwavering flak, the legislature passed the intensive management law in 1994 and amended it in 1998. The statute required the Alaska Board of Game to identify moose, caribou, and deer populations that were important sources of human food for Alaskans, set population objectives for them, and directed the Alaska Department of Fish and Game to institute intensive management efforts to improve numbers if a population fell below objective. Intensive management could mean habitat improvement or regulatory changes, but frequently (and probably most effectively) meant predator control of some sort.

People may disagree whether predator control really works or whether it is ethical to kill one species to benefit another, but this debate doesn't really occur in rural Alaska where the reality of the "circle of life" is a pretty one-sided discussion. So too is the support for the premise that the highest and best use of most big game populations is to provide a sustainable source of human sustenance. The debate mostly occurs among urban residents of strongly differing values, or between those charged with implementing differing legal mandates. Little can be said about the different individual values. They tend to follow the pattern of how people might view other significant issues like evolution, gun rights, or abortion—the most vocal advocates position themselves at far ends of the spectrum and engage in heated discussion. For those attempting to implement potentially conflicting legal guidance, the discussions are far different.

ADF&G managers are charged, by State law, to institute intensive management programs when certain ungulate numbers fall below population goals. So how does this work when 60 percent of the State is federally managed? Awkwardly. There is no legal conflict on Forest Service and BLM lands, but in the many ANILCA-created conservation system units managed by FWS and the National Park Service, there is. Legal purposes for which

the units are to be managed included maintaining fish and wildlife populations in their natural diversity. How then can significant control efforts be
undertaken to depress one species with the clear goal to elevate numbers of
another? Biologists, managers, and legal scholars have batted this around
considerably. The Park Service published a legal review concluding intensive
management efforts were in conflict with their mandates. FWS remained
silent and tried to walk the fence—each proposal would be evaluated on a
case-by-case basis, but notable attempts to undertake such programs (like
aerially gunning wolves on Unimak Island to help Southern Alaska Peninsula
Caribou) were struck down. As much as ADF&G was displeased with the
Park Service's position, they knew what is was. FWS was accused of offering a
light at the end of the tunnel only to turn it off when the tunnel was entered.

Somewhat ironically, the appreciation for the benefits of predator
control blossomed under federal management. Pre-statehood federal war-
dens were all about reducing predators as a primary part of their job. Over
time their apparent effectiveness may have created an expectation that later
became difficult to replicate. Depressed predator populations can definitely
create more game. Sometimes this can have catastrophic ecological effects
(by the prey species overpopulating and destroying their own habitat); such
results may be rarer in Alaska, but still are of utmost concern to managers.
Length and severity of winters are most likely the greatest limiting factors
affecting ungulate populations in the far north, but predation can be a significant factor too and is the only one managers have a potential to influence.

It wasn't just wolves and bears that pre-statehood wildlife managers
targeted. For a time there was even a bounty on Dolly Varden (believing them
detrimental for eating salmon eggs). It was discontinued when managers
realized a good number of the tails being turned in for bounties were actually from rainbow trout. The evolution of federal wildlife control in Alaska
is probably best illustrated by the bald eagle. Also viewed as a predator of
salmon at the time (as well as of furbearers and waterfowl), a bounty was
placed on bald eagles in Alaska from 1917 to 1953. Both feet of the bird
had to be turned in to collect fifty cents. It is hard to imagine the hard shift

in management direction when only a few decades later someone could be fined up to $100,000 for knowingly taking a bald eagle when it was protected under the Endangered Species Act. Non-game animals were starting to receive attention and protection as well as game species by this time as well and the ecological importance of all species was increasingly heralded.

Bounty systems fell out of favor in years to come for all species. Restrictions on poisoning came too. Equally important perhaps was the reduction in trapping. Rural trappers largely transitioned from sled dogs to snow machines—dogs could be fed dried fish; snow machines required gasoline and that was expensive. Along with fluctuating fur prices, lost income from bounties, and changes in demographics, the number of predators trapped each year diminished. By the time of statehood, predators had been depressed for decades, but in the years to follow, the changes would have logically expected to result in their increase. Early attempts by State managers to manage predators had some success, but by the 1970s, laws and attitudes were changing, and in 1980 ANILCA brought even more change. Counter to some popular opinion, ADF&G was not trying to kill everything with teeth and claws. It was, however, attempting to implement a legislated mandate and reduce predation on depressed ungulate populations most used by people for food. For many of those opposed to all predator control, the distinction was without merit.

A good look at the case history of brown bear management on the Kenai Peninsula demonstrates how rapidly things can change with species management direction. When I first moved to Alaska in the late 1970s, there was a fall and spring season every year on the Kenai, but bears weren't common and harvest was low. In 1999 ADF&G estimated that there were 277 brown bears on the Kenai and managed them conservatively. The management plan at the time estimated the population could be sustained if no more than 14 bears a year were taken, and no more than six could be mature females. Defense of life and property kills of bears often exceeding these numbers any given year, so regular hunting seasons frequently were suspended. In 2008, 40 bears died without hunting. Managers had been concerned that Kenai Peninsula bears were effectively cut off from the rest of Alaska, may be genetically distinct, and might deserve special management consideration similar to Yellowstone area grizzly bears—perhaps even protection as a threatened species. Managers were also in general agreement that the brown bear population was likely increasing at that time.

Getting an accurate estimate of bear numbers was not easy but clearly necessary to drive future management decisions. After an extended wrestling match fueled by state/federal authoritative differences, an extensive survey effort was undertaken for the Kenai Peninsula. The sampling regime employed the establishment of large grids, attraction sites with barbed wire to collect hair samples, DNA analyses of the hair, and a scientific-based mark/recapture estimation formula peer reviewed by leading experts. The results (2010) estimated 582 brown bears were calling the Kenai Peninsula home, with a 95 percent confidence that the true number was between 469 and 719.

Along with an increasing brown bear population and increased confidence in bear numbers, Kenai moose, particularly in Game Management Unit 15(A), were declining. Much of this area had benefited from large fires in 1947 and 1969 but had regrown to the point moose browse was limiting. Multiple research efforts had also clearly demonstrated that bears, both black and brown, were very significant predators of moose calves in their first month of life. Discussions commenced on how to apply intensive management to the Kenai. Some restrictions were placed on moose hunting and brown bear season was liberalized. In 2012 over 600 hunters took 44 brown bears, including 13 adult females. In 2013 the season was extended, and hunters for the first time could harvest a brown bear over bait. Seventy-one bears were taken, including 23 adult females. In 2014 the number was 69 total bears and six females. In less than three years approximately 200 brown bears had died on the Kenai, including those taken by hunters. The Refuge took exception to the mortality rate pointing out that under any management model such harvest was not sustainable. The biological discussions became political. The federal/state divide widened.

THERE IS SOMETHING ABOUT WOLVES

I don't know what it is about wolves that sets them apart for me. I have watched the wolf control debates and participated in countless discussions on the ecological importance and management of the species, but in my 30 years in Alaska, I never killed one. This might not sound odd, but for me it kind of was. Though I have softened some over the years, I was basically a strong participant in most of the consumptive uses throughout my career. I hunted, fished, and trapped—a lot. It is not that I thought wolves should not be killed—in fact I strongly believed they should be managed, but I never opted to be the one doing that kind of management. And it is not that I believed that the wolf was somehow my personal totem, though I have had many close encounters with the species that have left very strong personal impressions. I think it is because I love dogs, and I may see wolves pretty much as big, wild dogs. This emotion might best be illustrated by an event years ago that happened while I was staffing a waterfowl hunter check station on Hillside National Wildlife Refuge near Yazoo City, Mississippi. Mississippi was the only state in the Country at the time that allowed the use of dogs to hunt deer, but the practice was prohibited on the Refuge. In fact, staff were directed to shoot loose dogs found running on the Refuge to protect wildlife. While sitting in the small plywood shack with the door open one morning, I heard a slight stir. Looking down I saw a hound dog that would have made Bart Simpson's pup look like best in show. He was skin and bones, covered with mange, and had a piece of tattered baling twine growing out of his neck. I had a rifle and revolver and the humane thing would have probably been to put him out of his misery; instead I gave him my sandwich.

Opportunities to take wolves while hunting, trapping, or working in Alaska were numerous, but I never did. The first such time, I was hunting Dall sheep in the Alaska Range, creeping along looking for a band of rams I had spied the evening before. All of a sudden there was a serious commotion on the hillside ahead. A frantic ewe sheep was running and sliding down the scree slope and a large white wolf was directly behind, about to overtake her. I worked a round into my .270 and slipped off the safety aiming at the wolf's shoulder. I started to squeeze the trigger but stopped as the wolf halted its pursuit. We watched each other for a few moments and he turned and loped away. I did not fire. I rationalized to myself that the August pelt wasn't prime, or that the shot might scare the rams, or that I didn't want to carry a wolf hide and a sheep 15 miles out of the mountains, but it seemed to be more than that.

The most surreal experience with a wolf for me was on the trapline. I was following a moose trail along a frozen river to one of my fox sets. It was snowing lightly and there were no tracks of any kind evident in front of me as I approached a fallen tree where I had made the set. As I reached the log I jumped back. Immediately on the other side was a young wolf, laying down curled up, a front paw outstretch where it was held by several toes stuck in one of my 1.75 coil-spring traps. I reached into my parka and pulled out my .22 pistol and aimed at the animal's head. It didn't move. I didn't shoot. I looked around and found a long black spruce pole and approached the still motionless animal. Carefully, I depressed the trap's spring with the pole in one hand while trying to still aim at the wolf with my pistol in the other. It worked rather well, surprisingly, and the wolf pulled free and ran away quickly. It did not growl and barely struggled. Weird.

Shortly after moving to Cold Bay, I was driving a Refuge truck out to Grant Point at Izembek Lagoon and a group of wolves crossed the gravel road in front of me. Rather than speed up and high-tail it away from the vehicle, they turned and watched me, then one laid down. This is in an area where wolves are hunted throughout much of the year. That too seemed weird. A year or two later, I was checking the Cold Bay dump for wildlife carcasses when a wolf limped into view. It was badly wounded and was scavenging in the dump. I had my service revolver and probably should have shot the wolf but instead returned to the office and called around town looking for anyone who may have shot but not recovered a wolf recently. I made contact, told the person where the wolf was, and asked that he be the one to finish what he had started.

I have many more memories of wolf encounters, and frankly most behaved exactly as you would expect—with fear and an immediate interest in escape, yet there are enough memories of exchanging howls with a distant wolf from camp, or trading stares across the safety of a stream, that sets the animal apart in my mind from other creatures in the wilderness. They are special. They are also incredibly efficient predators and will kill old and young animals alike, wild and domestic. They are only doing what they were born to do. True wilderness would be a lesser place without them, but I would have never reintroduced them to the Lower 48 as FWS did in the 1990s. They are an animal of true wilderness and sadly most of the United States no longer has that quality. Putting wolves into small parks and wilderness areas is kind of like keeping elephants in concrete pens in zoos (my opinion); it's more bad than good. Wolves won't stay in small areas, they will kill livestock and pets, they will demand countless unproductive time of already over-taxed wildlife managers, and they will need to be managed which will be controversial to undertake and difficult to achieve. The first year or two of control efforts come relatively easy, but wolves are smart. Soon, liberal seasons and bag limits struggle to keep pace with the increase in numbers and wide dispersion that can be expected of wolves.

In all fairness, FWS initiated wolf reintroduction (into Yellowstone and Central Idaho) to try and jump-start recovery and save time and money. Wolves were slowly coming back into the mountain states from Canada and were protected under the Endangered Species Act. Calculated reintroduction could speed up the inevitable. The effort was quickly opposed by unlikely allies. Stock growers of course had concern, but so did some conservation interests. Their objection was that the reintroduced wolves were different that those that had been native, and presumably still existed in small numbers. Bringing in "outside" wolves could speed up the loss of the natural genetic integrity through hybridization. The courts batted the issue around for a few years, but ultimately the wolves were allowed to stay. Of course they didn't stay put—there are now identifiable packs in at least six western states from the two-state reintroduction effort. Three states have liberal hunting seasons now but the numbers continue to increase. I have a pack living only a few miles from where I retired in southwest Oregon. Some would call the results a success; others a travesty.

Predator management has changed significantly in the past few decades. Its challenges have continued to increase. The federal/state management differences in Alaska have fueled some of the controversy. Many people hold that State managers should have primary authority over management of all resident wildlife; others point out that federal parks and wildlife refuges belong to all Americans and the wildlife found therein should be managed accordingly. The federal supremacy for managing wildlife on federal lands has strong legal standing: landmark Supreme Court decisions gave deference to federal managers to both restrict a state from removing wildlife without permission from federal lands (*Kleppe* v. *New Mexico*) and to remove wildlife without state permission (*Hunt* v. *U.S.*). But just because the feds have the authority does not mean they should use it. I strongly believe there are too many conservation challenges, and too few conservation workers, for any of the workers to be at odds unnecessarily. Fundamentally the federal/state differences in Alaska could be resolved and all the players move on to play the rest of the game together. It is understandably a difficult task in the face of the dual subsistence management regime, which places enormous strain on federal/state relationships. The wrestling over authority is nothing new however. I recall a 1960 memo raising concern over an ADF&G proposal to kill sea lions off the rookeries at Forrester Island (a federal refuge) believing they had the authority to do so. They didn't, but they believed the new state was entitled to manage all of its fish and game as it chose. Many still believe that way.

A wolf watches the author pass.

Chapter Thirteen:
NEVER ALONE

It was day 11 on the river—the second day in a row of calm. In fact, the wind had laid down so much that the smoke from the active wildfires had settled in the river valley and visibility was near zero. It was peaceful but also created an eerie feeling—paddling on the expanse of flat water through thick, bluish-gray air. I joked with myself silently that I didn't really know whether I was paddling towards the Yukon Crossing, about 120 miles downstream, or back toward Canada. There was no visible current and the braided channels were over half a mile wide. I did have one sure indicator however, besides my compass. The sun produced a distinct glowing orb through the thick smoke, and that provided a target to move away from in the morning, and toward in the evening.

Many folks asked me at the onset of this trip, and many other solo adventures over the years, "You're not going alone are you?" My response, in later years has been, "I'm never alone." This wasn't meant to be coy, rather, it was because of a deep sense of being close to God when in wild country and away from distractions.

My spiritual belief in a Creator has not always been supported when interacting with fellow biologists. Then again, while always willing to converse about both the natural and supernatural, I tried to live by the tenets of my faith, but without striving to make everyone believe as I did. Many colleagues who engaged in such discussions held that the universe, and the life that dwelled within, was a mere artifact of time and chance and evolutionary processes. To me, atheism required more faith than I had. I did believe in biological processes that allowed better suited organisms—stronger or better adapted individuals of a species—a better chance of surviving and passing on their genes. I had not perceived however, any reasoned explanation for the existence of a planet such as earth, by chance, that supported life. Considering that the earth spins on its axis at approximately 1,000 mph, while rotating around the sun at about 67,000 mph while at a perfect distance from the sun to neither burn up or freeze the planet's life. Considering too that plant and animal life exist in a symbiotic balance that allows the other to survive—animals exhaling carbon dioxide which plants use, with sunlight, to produce oxygen and food that are necessary for animals to live. And even if by chance of a universal "big bang" the earth formed in a way to support life, and formed gravity so said life didn't hurl off into space, and that somehow lightning struck a primordial pool in just the right way to create the spark of life, how did it then reproduce itself? Ah, these are the kind of thoughts that go through one's mind when left alone in nature for days and weeks on end.

I had more acceptance of fellow scientists who held agnostic views. They generally believed God may exist but that it is not known, or may not even be possible to know. The truth of the matter is that the logic of a Creator is not a scientific concept. It cannot be tested in the natural world. Understanding that a Creator may best explain the unknowns of the universe does not set well with purely scientific thought where curiosity demands testing of theories and replication of results. It is however, the spark of a spiritualism than can provide answers to difficult questions, direction in life, a peaceful existence, and even eternal hope. When mulling over the universal question of, "What is the meaning of life?" perhaps one ought to also ponder the meaning of death. It seems to support no natural purpose other than to promote further life. I believe these answers are available to those who truly seek them and that a relationship with God, not just a belief in God, is what is so valuable. Such spiritual growth is difficult surrounded by noise and hustle and bustle of everyday life. It comes much more naturally when alone in wilderness for prolonged periods. I am reminded that even Jesus went alone into the wilderness for 40 days to pray to God the Father.

I remember my first real alone time growing up. I was 15 and since I was not able yet to drive myself, my mother dropped me off in the Cascade Mountains of Oregon for a week of what is now the Sky Lakes Wilderness Area. I had a backpack with camping gear and plenty of food, along with a fishing pole and rifle (it was bear season). About day three I was kind of bored, not wanting to hike any further, and having already caught enough trout for dinner. I basically was just laying back and waiting a couple of hours for dark to enjoy a campfire and then to lay in my sleeping bag and gaze up at the stars. While killing time mindlessly, however, I started to have a bit of an anxiety attack. I was a long ways off the trail and a long ways from any town and many days away from being picked up. A strange worry came over me that I could neither explain nor control. I sat for a while and pondered my state of mind and prayed. I do not remember an immediate change that afternoon. I do remember though, that for the nearly 50 years that followed, and more solo adventures than I can recall, I never felt anything but peace when being by myself in nature ever again. It has become something I long for and appreciate more and more the older I get.

As I paddled along in the still of the morning, I gave long thought to how I had transitioned from boyhood to a biologist, and then on to being a bureaucrat. I had no real regrets come to mind; the years had been good. I also mulled over my options of where I was right then. I had experienced five days of strong winds—day and night. It was calm now, but would it last? The air was thick with smoke, but tolerable to breathe, unlike a couple of nights where choking and coughing were the rule. Would that last too? The water was flat, with no visible current. I was going to have to work hard for each mile I paddled. Looking at the map, I knew the village of Beaver was a few miles ahead, on the north bank. Should I pull in there?

The river wandered through multiple twisted braids and I continued to hang to the right to keep my options open. When I had passed Circle many days earlier, I was nearly half a mile away when I saw the top of a crane, indicating human activity. I would not have been able to paddle back upstream to the community at that point if I wanted to. Fortunately I didn't care then. Now however, I was getting a stronger and stronger feeling I should pull in at Beaver, check the status of the various fires, and at least see what options existed for a scheduled flight to Fairbanks via a mail plane. I was about to pass an entrance to a slough on my right when I thought I heard the hum of a motor some distance ahead. I dug in the paddle hard on the left and entered the slough. As I progressed slowly the noise continued to grow. Nearly 40 minutes later I came to the boat landing at Beaver. I was less than 100 yards away before I could see anything through the smoke, but then immediately recognized movement from two people wearing bright yellow Nomex shirts. The source of the noise became clear too. The firefighters were tending a large pump which was sucking water out of the Yukon into a long hose line laid along the east side of the village. The men shut off the pump and disappeared up the hill as I beached the canoe.

I stopped at the first cabin up from the boat landing. A man was sitting on the porch railing and we exchanged pleasantries. He said that the BLM (Alaska Fire Service) had a large camp up at the airstrip and they could give me fire status information. He also said I should talk to his father about flights and motioned me into the cabin. There I met Paul Williams, Sr. Paul was an 82-year-old Gwich'in chief and elder. He asked if I wanted to go to Fairbanks and I responded affirmatively, having made up my mind that was the sensible thing to do. He made a call and reserved a seat on the plane scheduled later in the afternoon. He then invited me to sit and relax. My eyes wandered around the interior of the cabin and I spied family photos, a picture of a much younger Paul in a military uniform, an open Bible, and what looked to be old FWS uniform components. The conversation was slow at first but it quickly became apparent we had much in common, including our core beliefs and a shared history of working with FWS. Paul had been an employee of the Yukon Flats National Wildlife Refuge for 16 years and had been retired for ten. We knew a lot of the same people and had visited a lot of the same places. The minutes turned to hours and the hours to days. The scheduled plane was cancelled due to smoke, and would continue to be so for a few days. Paul graciously let me use a bunk in his cabin, fed me, and answered more questions than any host ought to have endure. We quickly became friends.

To kill time in the coming days, Paul took me around the village on his ATV and out on the river in his boat. We ate king salmon freshly pulled from a fish wheel. I spotted a wolf on shore on one outing and Paul howled at it while I attempted to take a picture. We talked about fish and wildlife, FWS, ANCSA, government, mutual acquaintances, and the weather. One afternoon, we were preparing to take some salmon heads and guts to the dump on Paul's ATV when Paul remarked, "Rain bird says it's going to rain." I had been following the weather forecast with the BLM folks carefully—thinking mostly about a hoped for wind shift that would allow the smoke to clear enough for a plane to land. I replied, "Yeah, there is a 20 percent chance of rain today." Paul didn't look up but softly said, "Rain bird says 100 percent chance." We hadn't been riding the ATV more than a few minutes and the first rain drop hit my forehead out of a smoky and otherwise unreadable sky.

Upon returning to Paul's cabin I asked him about rain birds. He said that we called them northern three-toed woodpeckers. Our conversations that afternoon were stimulated by a new appreciation I had for Paul's knowledge and manners. Too many times biologists pay little attention to traditional knowledge of Alaska Natives. Like all cultures, there are examples of superstitions and myths, but that said, there are far more examples of thousands of years of experiences and observations and knowledge passed down over generations. This connection to the land, animals, and weather has almost certainly been critical in the survival of people in incredibly harsh surroundings over time. The information should be cherished and not taken lightly. One discussion about wildlife lead to another, and then another. Perhaps for the first time ever I also became aware of the shared connection between all of God's creation—man and animals—in a way I had never considered. This revelation was more valuable than any other single memory from my Yukon River adventure. I gave Paul my canoe and assorted gear to do with as he chose. I also gave him an old rusty Remington shotgun. Paul said he would treasure it always. He also quizzed me about my heritage and said that I may be White, but that I had an Indian's heart. I don't think I had ever received a better or more heartfelt compliment. When finally departing, I shook his hand and then gave him a big hug. I wasn't sure whether such a gesture was ever comfortable for a White man or Indian, but it felt right.

Paul Williams, SR – Beaver, Alaska.

EPILOGUE

After several days of waiting for the smoke to clear enough for the scheduled mail plane to land in Beaver, the sky lightened up a bit and a Warbelow Air Navajo circled once and then came in low over the birch forest and landed on the gravel airstrip. There was a rush within the village to unload and load the plane before the conditions changed again and within minutes gear was weighed, stowed, and seven passengers and pilot were buckled in and speeding back down the strip and into the air. Within seconds we were above the cloud and smoke layer and visibility to the ground was again lost until nearly half way to Fairbanks. Barry Whitehill, retired FWS employee, a mutual friend of Paul Williams (and a former Assistant Refuge Manager of Yukon Flats National Wildlife Refuge), picked me up at the airport and graciously hosted me for the night at his home. That evening we attended a Borough Assembly meeting.

The Fairbanks North Star Borough Assembly was considering forming a task force for a planning effort to address climate change and the assembly chambers were packed with members of the public who wanted to testify. Predictably, the views were polarized. Some argued that climate change was rapidly changing the environment globally and very notably locally, and that ignoring the fact was irresponsible for a governing body. Others argued that the climate is always changing, climate science is unproven, and that a task force and planning effort would likely result in unnecessary government regulations and increase the cost of living with no foreseeable benefit. It was the less global, more local comments, however, that seemed to get the

Assembly's attention. One commenter, a union member and construction worker, didn't try to evaluate the legitimacy of climate science, but spoke to the reality of his business booming because of the growing number of home foundations failing due to melting permafrost. Another community member addressed the length of the fire season now versus decades past, again not debating cause and effect issues but the reality of what the community had to manage through. Regardless of cause, the new reality should be addressed by government in a thoughtful and logical fashion he shared, not left to chance, at least if there was anything that could be done. Barry spoke too. After retiring from FWS he went to work for FEMA with the understanding he would likely be called up rarely. Quite the opposite became the norm. The proliferation of natural disasters across the United States had offered regular work for him—more than he might prefer. Barry finished his testimony with something to the effect, "Mother Nature bats last, and she is stepping up to the plate." The resolution passed.

———————

While driving a rental car south the next day, I reflected on how Alaska had changed in the previous 40 years. The weather certainly was different. The political and social climates had changed too. I met up with Shannon in Anchorage and we visited with Alex and Jay and their two corgis before going on to the Kenai Peninsula to visit our other children, Rem and his wife Shelby, and Hannah and her husband Erik (plus our delightful granddaughter Eliza). The news was full of continuing financial woes for the State of Alaska, and of heated discussions over the future fate of the Alaska Permanent Fund Dividend (PFD). I remembered paying taxes when I first moved to Alaska, followed by their abolishment and replacement with a check from the state government annually to me rather than me sending a check sent to them. I had no complaints. Thirty years of investing PFD checks that came each year to every man, woman, and child were the reason we were able to put three children through college at the same time without taking out a loan. I remember too though, when the PFD program was initiated under Governor

Hammond's leadership, the State was swimming with extra oil money and had a hard time spending it all—building fish hatcheries across the State and even investing in gold. Money, surplus to the operational needs of the State under the PFD program, were to go to its citizens, the true owners of Alaska's rich resources. The PFD principle was also referred to as a "rainy day fund" to be used by government in the inevitable day that oil revenue declined; it after all was a non-renewable resource, unless you were willing to wait a few million years. And while some might argue that it wasn't raining yet, it certainly seemed to be sprinkling pretty hard and more nimbus clouds were forming on the horizon.

Rem worked for a Native Corporation on the North Slope and Alex for an engineering firm in Alaska. Their jobs were being less affected by the State's financial woes than Hannah's, though neither would likely have the positions they held without the oil and gas industry. Oil was the life blood of the State. Hannah, like her mother, had chosen to be a school teacher, and impacts to public schools and the university system, along with public roads maintenance, and changes to public safety, seemed most evident to me. An indirect result of eroding public program financial support was most glaring when we visited our Kenai Peninsula cabin. When we moved away in 2009 we could not imagine not having a place to call our own in the state we considered our home—our children were still there and we would visit often. We had a comfortable two-story cabin framed up on a couple of acres overlooking Cook Inlet with spectacular views of the Alaska Peninsula and Alaska Range. In the first year of retirement we spent months finishing the cabin with our friend David Mathiesen only to have much of our work destroyed by thieves who broke in a short time after we left. Not ready to abandon our dream, we restocked and secured the following summer making sure to have nothing of extreme value there to tempt a potential thief. No matter—the next time our cabin was ransacked, the thieves took everything, including my easy chair and the wood stove. After losing thousands of dollars of uninsured furnishings and recreational items we had had enough and put the cabin on the market. Unsold, Shannon and I visited the cabin for a couple of days, camping out in its remaining Spartan environment, and lamenting over changes in Alaska and a dream lost.

When we first moved to Alaska, crime was rare—you could leave your home unlocked and not worry about its contents disappearing. People didn't break into a cabin unless they found themselves in an emergency and then they would likely seek out the owner later and make things right. Over time, the State had grown and a portion of its populace had changed. The lack of government funding also necessitated tough budget decisions. It takes money to catch thieves, money to prosecute them, and even more money to incarcerate them for any real length of time. Higher priority crimes took precedent and as deterrents to other lesser crimes diminished, the occurrence of those lesser crimes increased. It wasn't rocket science.

My sister Jean flew to Anchorage and joined me for the drive back down the Alaska Highway to Oregon. Nearly 3,000 miles of driving together is a great way to catch up on whatever topic comes to mind, and if conversation wanes, it is a great time to listen to books on tape.

After arriving home I packed up again and headed to the Eagle Cap Wilderness in northeastern Oregon, longbow in hand, and in pursuit of the winter's meat supply. Jim Akenson, and Penny, Bird, and Bat (wilderness savvy pack mules) helped pack my elk back to my vehicle and a few days later the meat was cut, wrapped, and in the freezer. A couple months went by before the next adventure—in the Cabeza Prieta Wilderness on the border of Arizona and Mexico. There I was in pursuit of desert bighorn sheep, a once-in-a-lifetime opportunity, if one is fortunate enough to draw a tag in the first place. It took 28 years of applying, and 73 miles of backpacking in the Sonoran Desert before I was successful.

I took time out to write this book, not for want of places to go, but due to the abundance of caution directed toward the entire nation during the Coronavirus outbreak, and the rules for social distancing and avoidance of discretionary travel. I can see nothing positive in the pandemic, other than it created the time to sit down and do some writing—I suspect others too have found themselves completing projects that they otherwise never would have undertaken. Another possible plus could be an awakening for some of just how fragile human life can be. It is important to never lose sight of that. Now, in finishing this book, I begin to plan another backpacking trip this coming fall, this time into an area I hunted and explored with my father many years ago, deep in the Frank Church—River of No Return Wilderness in central Idaho. Lord willing I will undertake this adventure, and perhaps many more. I know though, if I never travel again to remote and wild places I cannot complain. I have traveled to all 50 states and to nearly 30 countries on six continents. I have seen the northern lights and the southern lights. I have slept in ice caves and climbed mountains. I have shared sunrises and campfires with family and friends. And I have spent 30 of the past 40 years living and working in one of the most incredible places on the planet, and have just seen The Country one more time, and it was good.